Justices of the Supreme Court

JOHN MARSHALL

The Great Chief Justice

Barbara Silberdick Feinberg

ENSLOW PUBLISHERS, INC.

44 Fadem Road	P.O. Box 38
Box 699	Aldershot
Springfield, N.J. 07081	Hants GU12 6BP
U.S.A.	U.K.

J B Marshall

Dedication

In memory of Ruth Lippman, a remarkable woman.

Acknowledgments

I would like to thank the following people who helped me locate information and photographs for this biography of John Marshall:

Irving Adleman, Assistant Director, Head of Reference, East Meadow Public Library; Marilyn Bunshaft, Community Affairs Officer, East Meadow Public Library; Margaret Cook, Curator of Manuscripts and Rare Books, Swem Library, College of William and Mary; Suzanne Freedman, freelance researcher; Elizabeth Stanton Kostelny, Curator of Collections, the Association for the Preservation of Virginia Antiquities; and my aunt, Estelle Stiebel of Richmond, Virginia.

Library of Congress Cataloging-in-Publication Data

Feinberg, Barbara Silberdick.
    John Marshall: The Great Chief Justice / Barbara Silberdick Feinberg.
       p.   cm.— (Justices of the Supreme Court)
    Includes bibliographical references and index.
    ISBN 0-89490-559-7
    1. Marshall, John, 1755-1835—Juvenile literature. 2. Judges—United States—Biography—Juvenile literature. [1. Marshall, John, 1755–1835. 2. Judges. 3. United States. Supreme Court—Biography.] I. Title. II. Series.
KF8745.M3F4 1995
347.73'2634—dc20
[B]
[347.3072634]
[B]   94-31489
                                   CIP
                                   AC

Printed in the United States of America

10 9 8 7 6 5 4 3 2 1

Photo Credits: Courtesy of the Architect of the Senate, p. 93; Courtesy of the Association for the Preservation of Virginia Antiquities, pp. 26, 28, 31, 47, 49, 68, 74, 83, 91; Courtesy of Bettman Archives, p. 61; Courtesy of Swem Library, College of William and Mary, pp. 24, 45; Franz Jantzen, "From the Collection of the Supreme Court of the United States", p. 95; From the Collection of the Supreme Court of the United States, pp. 9, 13; Reproduced from the Collections of the Library of Congress, p. 59.

Cover Photo: Association for the Preservation of Virginia Antiquities

⚖ CONTENTS ⚖

1

The Case of the "Midnight Judge"

Forty-one-year-old William Marbury was promised a new government job. He had once worked for the first Secretary of the Navy, Benjamin Stoddert. Then, President John Adams, serving his final days in office, offered to make Marbury a justice of the peace for the District of Columbia. Justices of the peace settled minor legal disputes and issued court orders. To make his appointment official, Marbury needed a commission, a government document naming him to the post. Little did he know how difficult it would be to get that commission.

On March 3, 1801, his last night as president, John Adams sat at his desk signing documents at a furious pace.[1] He was busy appointing his supporters to the federal courts. Among the documents on his desk was Marbury's commission. By nine o'clock, Adams hastily finished his work and went to bed. (In the days to come, however, Adams's political opponents would ridicule his last-minute appointees by calling them "the midnight judges.") While Adams slept, clerks brought the signed commissions to Secretary of State John Marshall. He attached the Great Seal of the United States to the documents to make them official. Then they were ready to be distributed. There were, however, too many commissions and too little time to deliver them. Some were sent out, but others, including Marbury's were not.

The next morning, Marshall's brother James, himself a new judge, volunteered to hand out some of the remaining commissions on his way back to his home in Virginia. He signed a receipt for a package of documents. The package, however, was too bulky for him to manage. So he removed some of the commissions, gave them back to the State Department, and crossed them off the receipt. Among these was Marbury's official appointment. It was never delivered. In a private latter, John Marshall later wrote: "I fear some blame may be imputed to me . . . I should have sent out the commissions which had been signed & sealed but for the extreme hurry of the time and the absence of Mr. Wagner [his clerk] who had been called on by the President to act as his private secretary."[2]

Marbury's appointment was one example of the struggle between the nation's first two political parties for control of the federal courts. (Political parties put up candidates for office at election time. They often have different views about the way government should be run.) Thomas Jefferson's victorious Republican party had thoroughly defeated John Adams's Federalist party in the elections of 1800. The Republicans won the presidency and occupied most of the seats in Congress, the nation's lawmaking body. Adams had tried to prevent Republicans from serving on the nation's courts as well. That is why he appointed ninety-three Federalist "midnight judges," including Marbury, shortly before he left office.[3] The Judiciary Act of 1801 made it possible for him to do this.

Adams had signed the Judiciary Act on February 13 to keep the nation's courts under Federalist control. It increased the number of national circuit courts (federal courts that hear appeals from trial courts). The circuit courts were previously staffed by members of the Supreme Court, the highest court in the land. Now they would be replaced by new circuit court judges. Another law let him appoint more justices of the peace for the District of Columbia. This is why he had offered Marbury a job.

Why was Adams so determined to fill the courts with loyal Federalists? The Federalist party had governed the nation for twelve years, but Jefferson's Republicans promised to reverse much of what the Federalists had done. Instead of further strengthening the national government, the Republicans wanted to return some of its powers to the states. Rather than encouraging the growth of American businesses, they were more interested in developing the nation's farms. Instead of relying on property owners to vote for their leaders in government, the Republicans urged ordinary people to participate actively in politics. The courts offered Federalists their last chance to block or slow down the changes Jefferson and his supporters wanted to make.

Once they were in office, President Jefferson and the Republicans in Congress took steps to weaken the Federalists' control of the courts. The lawmakers set to work on a new law to reorganize the courts. Meanwhile, Jefferson let many of Adams's appointees stay at their posts, but he reduced the number of new justices of the peace from forty-two to thirty.

After all, the District of Columbia had a small population and did not need so many local officials. As a result, Marbury lost his promised job. Then the president ordered new commissions sent out to his appointees. At this point, the undelivered commissions Adams had signed were probably destroyed.

Ten months later, Marbury and three other disappointed "midnight judges" brought a lawsuit against Jefferson's secretary of state, James Madison, to get their commissions. It is not known why they waited so long before they acted. In the lawsuit, they asked the Supreme Court for a *writ of mandamus.* This is a court order requiring a government official to perform his lawful duties. It would compel Madison to give Marbury and the others their official papers. In December 1801, John Marshall, now Chief Justice of the United States (the head of the Supreme Court), and the rest of the Court agreed to hear the case.

To prepare for the lawsuit, Marbury needed proof that he had indeed been appointed a justice of the peace. He went to the State Department and asked James Madison about his commission. Had it actually been signed? Madison did not know. When Marbury demanded to see the document, he was turned over to Marshall's former clerk Jacob Wagner, still at work in the department. Wagner gave Marbury some disappointing news. The commissions were no longer in the State Department files. In desperation, Marbury turned to the senate for help. According to the Constitution,[4] senate approval was required for his presidential appointment. There would be records of the vote that Marbury could use. The Republican Senate, however, refused to cooperate with him. Then Marbury decided to take his case to the Supreme Court,

William Marbury, shown here in a portrait by Rembrandt Peale, was one of four disappointed "midnight judges" who brought a lawsuit against James Madison in order to receive his commission.

but he had to wait more than a year for the case to be heard. The Republicans were responsible for the delay.

Under Jefferson's leadership, the Republican Congress had struck back at the Federalist controlled courts. The lawmakers passed the Repeal Act in March 1802, canceling the Judiciary Act of 1801. Gone were the additional circuit courts and their newly appointed judges. Once again, members of the Supreme Court were assigned to the circuit courts. Marshall asked his fellow Justices not to serve on these courts, but they turned him down.[5] Until 1801, they had decided circuit court cases. They could offer no legal objections to taking up this duty once again.[6]

Adams's circuit court judges were supposed to hold office for life. They refused to be dismissed. The Republican Congress, however, refused to help them keep their posts. Then the individual judges sued the government. The trial courts ruled that they could not get their jobs back. The courts reasoned that the Constitution gives Congress the right to make changes in the court system. The cases were never appealed. If they had, Marshall would probably have supported the circuit judges' claims.[7]

In April 1802, the Republican Congress passed another law affecting the federal courts. The lawmakers had feared that the ousted circuit judges would bring their complaint before the Supreme Court. To delay possible action on the case, they eliminated the January and June sessions of the Supreme Court. The Court would meet only once a year, in February.[8] The Justices would not hear cases again until 1803. Because of this Marbury had to wait more than a year for a decision from the Supreme Court about his lawsuit against Madison.

During that time, attacks on the courts increased. The

Republican lawmakers tried to remove other Federalist judges from their posts. To change the judges each time a different political party came to power in the government would destroy the impartiality and independence of the nation's courts. Judgeships would become a political prize for whichever party won the elections. To prevent this, the nation's judges were supposed to hold office for life.

During the debates on the Repeal Act, some representatives urged Congress to replace Chief Justice Marshall with a Republican. The threat was never carried out. Early in 1802, however, the House of Representatives voted to bring charges against Federal District Judge John Pickering of New Hampshire, a very vulnerable target. Judge Pickering was a drunkard. He was also insane. Nevertheless, the Constitution only allowed a judge to be removed from office on grounds of "Treason [betraying one's country], Bribery [taking money for doing a political favor], or other high Crimes and Misdemeanors."[9] It took some twisting of the meaning of these words for the Senate to remove the incompetent judge on March 4, 1804. Later, Congress took steps to remove Supreme Court Justice Samuel Chase of Maryland. The attempt failed.

Meanwhile, on February 9, 1803, the Supreme Court heard its first case since 1801, Marbury's request for his undelivered commission. Faced with Republican threats to remove him and other Federalist judges, Chief Justice Marshall could have retreated under pressure. He could have dismissed the lawsuit or disqualified himself. By then, the trial seemed to be a waste of time because Marbury's unserved five-year term as justice of the peace was almost over. Also, there were grounds for the Chief Justice to withdraw from the case. After all, Secretary of State Marshall had originally

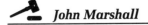

caused the problem by failing to delivery Marbury's commission.

What's more, no official appeared to defend Madison. Jefferson and his supporters had decided to ignore this unimportant case. Overconfident, they had underestimated Marshall. *Marbury* v. *Madison* would give Marshall the opportunity to put the Republicans in their place. It also would help him protect the nation's courts from further political attacks. For these reasons, John Marshall chose to hear the case.

Marbury's lawyer was Charles Lee. Lee, a friend of Marshall's, had served as both George Washington's and John Adams's attorney general. (Attorneys general argue the government's side in lawsuits.) The difficult task of proving Marbury's claim fell to him. He had to show that the missing commission had been properly signed and sealed before President Adams left office. Only then could Madison be compelled to deliver it. Lee questioned two reluctant state department clerks, Jacob Wagner and Daniel Brent, in court. They did not want to discuss matters affecting their department. Marshall ordered them to testify. Then they admitted that they did not know what had happened to Marbury's commission.

Next Lee called in Jefferson's Attorney General Levi Lincoln because he had served temporarily as secretary of state until James Madison arrived in Washington. Lincoln asked to have Lee's questions written down. He wanted to study them before supplying answers. He was caught between opposing interests. As a lawyer, he respected the court's need for information to decide a case. As Jefferson's attorney general, he was responsible to the president and would not embarrass him. Finally, he admitted that he could not

James Madison's failure to deliver commissions to John Adams's appointees led to the case of *Marbury* v. *Madison*. The government offered no defense of Madison's inaction. Apparently, Thomas Jefferson and his supporters had decided to ignore this case as unimportant.

remember the names on the missing commissions. He also testified that he did not give the commissions to Madison. Lee then presented sworn statements from a third State Department clerk and from James Marshall to prove that Marbury's commission had been properly signed and sealed. The Court could order Madison to deliver it.

Once this evidence was presented, it was the Chief Justice's turn to act. John Marshall had a dilemma. He could deny Marbury's request for a court order. Then, the Republican triumph over the courts would be complete. On the other hand, he could rule in Marbury's favor. However, he would still have no way of forcing Madison to give Marbury his commission. The solution John Marshall thought up was ingenious. It turned an unimportant case about a "midnight judge" into a landmark decision.

A Virginian Becomes An American

John Marshall was a remarkable man. Despite little formal schooling or training as a lawyer, he became an outstanding Chief Justice of the Supreme Court. He is remembered for the landmark cases he decided. John Marshall was, however, a private individual as well as a public figure. His personal life was filled with adventure, romance, and drama.

John Marshall was born in a tiny log cabin in Germantown in Prince William County, Virginia, on September 24, 1755. He grew up in Virginia's backwoods. The nearest neighbors lived miles away, but he had plenty of company. He was the eldest of fifteen children. Amazingly, his eight sisters and six brothers had all survived to become adults. In colonial America, it was unfortunately all too common for babies to sicken and die shortly after their birth.

During Marshall's youth, his father, Thomas Marshall, frequently traveled around Virginia. He was a surveyor, like his friend George Washington. Washington had hired Thomas Marshall to help map lands belonging to Lord Fairfax. Thomas Marshall was also a member of the Virginia House of Burgesses, a group of lawmakers, meeting in distant Williamsburg, the colony's capital. Over the years, Thomas Marshall became successful buying and selling land. He moved his family to a four-room house in Fauquier County, close to the Blue Ridge Mountains. In 1773, he and his sons started building Oak Hill, a seven-room frame house, with the first glass windows in the county. In 1783, John Marshall's parents and their younger children moved on to a part of Virginia, which later became the state of Kentucky. Upon his death in 1803, Thomas Marshall left Oak Hill to John, who spent most summers of his adult life there.

John Marshall's mother Mary Randolph Keith, a distant cousin of Thomas Jefferson, busily tended her growing brood of children. Unlike most colonial women, she was able to read and write. She taught their children herself until Scottish minister Reverend James Thomson arrived in the parish in 1767. He lived with the family for a year. The minister instructed John Marshall in Latin as well as other subjects. By this time, Marshall had also read Shakespeare, Dryden, and other works of English literature. When Reverend Thomson left, John Marshall's parents decided to send him to Reverend Archibald Campbell's academy, one hundred miles away. During the year Marshall spent at the academy, he became friends with future president James Monroe.

When John Marshall returned home, he read the Blackstone's *Commentaries on the Laws of England,* first published in the colonies in 1772. Perhaps, this important book about English law led Marshall to become a lawyer. As was common in those days, he learned to be a lawyer by working at an attorney's office in town. It was ten miles away, and he traveled the distance on foot. Fortunately, he enjoyed long walks. On his way, he would often meet people and swap stories with them.[1] Concentrating on his legal studies, however, proved difficult for the eighteen year old. He knew that war with Britain was coming, and he was already preparing himself to fight.[2]

Throughout his childhood, John Marshall had listened carefully as his father described the colonists' lists of complaints against Britain. As a lawmaker, Thomas Marshall knew firsthand that British policies were hurting the colonies. He explained to his children how the Proclamation of 1763 had kept Virginians from expanding westward. John Marshall learned that his father had met with other patriots at Raleigh Tavern to vote against the Stamp Act of 1765. The act would have made colonists pay a fee every time they needed a legal document, bought a newspaper, or purchased a pack of playing cards. The Marshalls sympathized with the people of New England when the British Intolerable Acts closed the port of Boston in 1774.[3] In April 1775, word reached Virginia that minutemen were fighting the British at Concord and Lexington. John Marshall immediately followed his father into the Virginia militia. By then, the Virginia colonists had their own problems with the British. Royalist Governor Lord Dunmore seized supplies of gunpowder stored in Williamsburg. He threatened to free all the slaves to help put down any uprising the colonists might be planning.

Nineteen-year-old lieutenant John Marshall took charge of training volunteers for his community. He was already six feet tall, with a round face, penetrating dark eyes, and a mop of black hair. A kinsman who was there described Marshall's first meeting with the volunteers:

> He proceeded to inform the company . . . that he had come to meet them as fellow-soldiers, who were likely to be called on to defend their country and their own rights and liberties, . . . that there had been a battle at Lexington, in Massachusetts, between the British and Americans, in which the Americans were victorious, but that more fighting was expected; . . .
>
> He went through the manual exercise, by word and motion, deliberately pronounced and performed in the presence of the company, before he required the men to imitate him; and then proceeded to exercise them with the most perfect temper.[4]

After the training session, the company broke up to play games and race each other. As the local footrace champion, Marshall earned their respect. At the end of the day, he walked ten miles back to his home.

In October 1775, Lord Dunmore directed the British navy to raid the Virginia coastline. The British fleet was based at Norfolk, the largest port city in the state. In November, the governor put the state under military rule. Anyone who opposed him was labeled a traitor. Nevertheless, the colonists prepared to fight. Marshall's regiment was alerted by a message from Patrick Henry, the patriotic colonial spokesman and soon, the first governor of Virginia. The men assembled at the village of Culpeper. Dressed in their deerskin trousers, with tomahawks attached to their belts and wearing colorful shirts embroidered with Patrick Henry's famous slogan "Liberty or death," the Culpeper Minutemen marched toward Norfolk to meet the British redcoats.

On the outskirts of the city, at Great Bridge, they dug in.

On December 9, the British attacked them. According to Marshall, the inexperienced but "bravest of Americans rushed to the works, where, unmindful of order, they kept up tremendous fire on the front of the British column."[5] The Minutemen defeated a combined force of more than five hundred British troops, loyalists, and slaves. Then they pushed on to Norfolk. Unfortunately, they could not protect the city from a terrible pounding by the British navy, or fires set by the retreating forces that burned it to the ground. With Norfolk destroyed, Dunmore was left without a base for his fleet. So Virginia was saved from British occupation.

Marshall returned home and described his first exploits under fire to his younger brothers and sisters. He did not remain home for long, however. In July 1776, he became a lieutenant in the Third Virginia Regiment of the Continental Army. He saw action at the battle of Brandywine with his unit under the command of the Marquis de Lafayette in September, 1777. This Frenchman was one of the European aristocrats fighting for American independence. Marshall was wounded in the hand at the battle of Germantown the following month.

Winter of 1777–1778 found Marshall with George Washington's troops at Valley Forge. It was here that he first met Alexander Hamilton, Washington's future secretary of the Treasury, and spent time with his former schoolmate, James Monroe. The soldiers were crowded into rude log huts where they huddled together for warmth. The officers ate potatoes, hickory nuts, bread, and an occasional piece of meat. The men had to make do with a watery soup and "fire cake," a horrible concoction of meal, water, leaves, and ashes.[6] With the absence of sanitation, diseases spread rampantly through the camp leaving only about a third of the men fit for duty. Marshall himself had only one shirt and a single blanket. When the shirt was washed, he had to wrap himself in the blanket to keep from freezing. Despite the deplorable conditions, he managed to stay healthy.

Marshall was named Deputy Judge Advocate. He was responsible for handling cases of military discipline and settling minor disputes among the starving, ragged, and ailing men. Serving with him at Valley Forge, Captain Philip Slaughter wrote that he was "an excellent companion, and idolized by the soldiers and his brother officers."[7] He kept up the men's spirits by telling them amusing stories and organizing activities. Marshall earned the nickname "Silverheels." This was not only because he won so many footraces in his stocking feet but because his mother had knit white heels into the blue socks she made for him.

After shivering through the winter at Valley Forge, Marshall found himself sweltering in one hundred-degree heat in June 1778 as a light infantryman at the battle of Monmouth. In December 1779, he was ordered back to Virginia to recruit troops to replace the men whose time was up. General Washington's army was a random collection of colonists, assembled by the individual states. The men served for a short time and then returned to their farms to plant or harvest crops. Marshall was part of an army that was poorly fed, badly trained, and ill-equipped. He regretted that the Continental Congress could only appeal to the states for support. It could not order the states to provide the supplies and men it needed.[8]

While waiting for the Virginian lawmakers to summon more men, John Marshall visited his father in Yorktown. In May 1780, after further delays, he decided to study law at the College of William and Mary, twelve miles away in

Williamsburg. He spent three months attending Chancellor George Wythe's classes. Wythe lectured and questioned students on readings from English law books. The developing American legal system was based on English law. A couple of times each month, the chancellor encouraged his students to practice their skills by arguing cases before him and the other professors. He also held mock lawmaking sessions to train his students in government. At William and Mary, Marshall joined Phi Beta Kappa, a college honor society, and improved his debating skills. At one of the meetings, John Marshall met Bushrod Washington, George Washington's nephew and a future Supreme Court Justice.

Marshall applied for a license to practice law in Fauquier County. It was signed by Governor Thomas Jefferson on August 28, 1780. Marshall was eager to start earning his own living. Nevertheless, that autumn, he walked all the way to Philadelphia to get vaccinated against smallpox once again. An earlier inoculation, given to him in Philadelphia in 1777, did not take, and it was illegal to get a vaccination in Virginia. There and back, he averaged 30 to 35 miles a day. After all the walking he had done in his youth, the distance between Virginia and Pennsylvania did not discourage him from going to get the vaccination.

In January 1781, American traitor Benedict Arnold, who became a British general, led his troups against Virginia. He sailed up the James River with the British fleet to invade Richmond, the new state capital. Governor Jefferson and many patriot families fled when Arnold's troops landed only thirty miles away. Marshall immediately rejoined the army and took command of a militia unit. They managed to ambush a British raiding party. They failed, however, to keep Arnold from reaching Richmond. He burned the city's arsenal, tobacco warehouses, and ships before he retreated. Marshall stayed in the army until February 12, 1781. Then he left to return to his law practice. In October, Washington defeated the commander of the British forces, Lord Cornwallis, at Yorktown.

John Marshall's experiences during the American Revolution helped to shape his attitudes toward government. Until he joined the Continental Army, he had never been away from his home state. Now he had a broader view of the colonies and the men who fought for their independence. Marshall became a nationalist. He viewed his new nation as a whole, not just from the perspective of his own state. His wartime experiences left him disappointed with the way the states had recruited and supplied the army. Like George Washington and Alexander Hamilton, he wanted the United States to form a strong national government with the power to take decisive action.

The War of Independence not only widened John Marshall's outlook on politics but also, in a round-about way, brought him a wife. Throughout the conflict, he had written letters to his father. They included descriptions of the action he had seen, anecdotes about army life, and fond messages for his sisters and brothers. Thomas Marshall, stationed in Yorktown, Virginia, since February 1778, was a colonel in command of the Virginia State Artillery. He proudly shared his son's letters with his friends, including Jacquelin Ambler, a member of the state government, Ambler's wife, and their four daughters.

Shortly after Christmas 1779, John Marshall arrived in Yorktown to see his father. From his parent's glowing praises, the Ambler sisters had expected to meet Prince Charming. The oldest sister, Eliza, wrote, "We had been accustomed to hear him spoken of by all as a very paragon [a model of excellence or perfection]; we had often seen letters from him fraught with filial and paternal affection."[9] Then in walked a disheveled backwoodsman with "awkward figure, unpolished manners, and total negligence of person."[10] Eliza was disappointed by Marshall's appearance, but her younger sister Mary Willis Ambler, called Polly, was impressed by his hearty laugh and funny stories. She shyly hid behind her sisters and listened to him. She quickly decided she wanted to marry him someday.[11]

Just before her fourteenth birthday, they were formally introduced at a ball. Wearing a much too large, hand-me-down blue gown and silver flowers in her brown curly hair, Polly Ambler was escorted by her family. Unlike her sisters, she had not yet taken dancing lessons. Nevertheless, she and Marshall managed to make their way around the floor without mishap. John Marshall later wrote, "I saw her first the week she attained the age of fourteen & was greatly pleased with her. Girls then came into company much earlier than at present."[12] For the next month, he visited the family, entertaining the girls by reading poetry and novels to them. Then he left to study law in Williamsburg.

Marshall could not stop thinking about Polly Ambler. He scribbled her name all over the two hundred pages of law notes he took. He even managed to leave his studies to return to Yorktown for visits. Before long, Polly's father's official duties required him and his family to move to Richmond. In June 1780, the family stopped off at Williamsburg to visit Marshall. There, they attended another ball, where John Marshall devoted himself to Polly. He decided to help the Amblers move into their new home before he returned to his military duties. Before long, the Amblers and other Richmond

23

This page from John Marshall's law notes, written in 1780, shows Polly Ambler's name scribbled all over it. Marshall could not stop thinking about Polly Ambler. He scribbled her name all over the two hundred pages of law notes he took.

families had to flee the city with the approach of Benedict Arnold's forces.

When they returned to Richmond in the spring of 1781, Marshall's regiment was disbanded. He began setting up his law practice. For the next year, he pursued Polly Ambler, writing her letters and visiting her home. He was jealous of the other men who came to see her. Marshall proposed to Polly at the end of the year, but she refused his offer. Perhaps she was following the custom that a woman should not accept the first time a man asked her to marry him. Perhaps she was uncertain. When Marshall immediately rode off, Polly began to cry. She realized that she had made a terrible mistake.[13] She persuaded her cousin to ride after Marshall to make him return. As proof of her sincerity, she snipped off a piece of her hair for her cousin to take to him. For the rest of her life, Polly Ambler wore a locket with the cutting of hair that brought John Marshall back to her.

They were married at the estate of her cousin John Ambler in Hanover County on January 3, 1783, two months before Polly's seventeenth birthday. The twenty-seven-year-old groom and his bride took their vows by candlelight before the Marshall and Ambler families, various government officials, and other guests. After the ceremonies, the wedding party sat down to a festive supper. Toasts were made to the new couple and then everyone danced. Returning to Richmond, John and Polly Marshall settled into a two-room rented cottage near the Ambler home. They started married life with hardly any money. They did own a slave and three horses; the horses were a gift from Thomas Marshall. The future, however, looked bright for John Marshall. He was already a state lawmaker.

Marshall often invited fellow lawmakers home for dinner.

Polly Ambler and John Marshall were married on January 3, 1783. Polly's wedding gown was made of patterned white silk. It was worn by many of her descendants, so the style was altered to suit the style of the time for later brides. The original gown probably had a pointed bodice and straight sleeves.

He and Polly entertained such notable Virginians as Patrick Henry, James Madison, and James Monroe. Frequently, the men discussed the shortcomings of the new Articles of Confederation, the nation's first constitution. Under the Articles, the states were loosely joined together. They kept the power to raise taxes and control trade for themselves. The national government could do little without their consent. Marshall's guests calmly debated whether the Articles should be improved or changed. He preferred change: "The general tendency of State politics convinced me that no safe and permanent remedy could be found, but in a more efficient and better organized general government."[14]

By 1790, Marshall was wealthy enough to build his wife a large home in Richmond with a dining room that could seat as many as thirty-two guests for dinner. Formal meals at the Marshall home were usually served at three o'clock in the afternoon. The table held pastries, blanc mange (a molded mixture of milk and gelatin), dishes of mutton, a roast turkey, potato pudding, and bowls of raisins, nuts, and oranges. Marshall thought his wife was an excellent housekeeper. She spent about three hours a day supervising her servants in the laundry, the nursery, and the kitchen.[15] In her spare time, she enjoyed playing cards and gossiping with other ladies.

In public, Polly Marshall was a quiet woman. In private, she would read the daily newspapers and discuss current events with her husband. He noted that her "timidity so influenced her manners that I could rarely prevail on her to display in company the talents I knew her to possess. They were reserved for her husband & her select friends."[16] Marshall added that "she possessed a good deal of chaste, delicate & playful wit, and, if she permitted herself to indulge this talent, told her little story with grace and could mimic

The John Marshall House, built in Federal style, was completed in 1790. On the first floor there are four rooms, the Great Hall, where the Marshalls entertained, a family dining room, a parlor, and a room most likely used by the servants. In 1805 a fifth room was added for Mrs. Marshall's nurse/companion. There were three bedrooms upstairs and a small storage area where the slaves may have slept. There was also an attic and a basement. Originally the house took up an entire city block. It had a kitchen, laundry, and smokehouse behind the main building. The stables were in a far corner of the lot. Marshall also had a separate two-story office on the property. The John Marshall house is located in Richmond, Virginia, and is open to visitors. It contains many objects that belonged to Chief Justice Marshall and his family.

very successfully the peculiarities of the person who was the subject."[17]

Between 1784–1805, Polly Marshall gave birth to ten children. Four died before they reached their teens. Tragically, in 1786, she developed a lifelong phobia, an overwhelming fear of sudden noises. That year, she lost her second child five days after its birth and suffered a miscarriage several months later. Her concerned and caring husband did his best to comfort her. Marshall moved his law office to another building on their property to keep her from being disturbed. His wife's reaction to noises prompted him to write a sad letter to a neighbor. "The distressed, I might say distracted, situation of my wife at length forces me very reluctantly to make a direct application to you . . . . The incessant barking of your dog has scarcely left her a night of quiet since the beginning of the summer."[18] The city officials even cooperated by not ringing the church bells on her worst days. Many of the letters Marshall wrote to her, when he was away from home, encouraged her to feel better. "Good health will produce good spirits & I wou'd not on any consideration relinquish the hope that you will possess both."[19] Always delicate, Polly Marshall, however, remained an invalid for the rest of her life.

Because of her illness, John Marshall frequently looked after the children, with help from family and servants. After the birth of a son, in 1798, Polly suffered from severe depression. She went to visit her sister Elizabeth, leaving the children behind. Marshall wrote her a touching letter about them. "Your sweet little Mary is one of the most fascinating creatures I ever beheld. . . . Poor little John is cutting teeth and of course is sick."[20] She recovered from this bout of mental illness, only to become depressed again in 1808.

After he became Chief Justice of the Supreme Court, Marshall still spent time with his children. He could often be found sitting on a bench beneath a huge oak tree in the yard of their home, surrounded by his young ones. He would think about the cases he had to decide. The children could not play noisily because their mother was ill. Yet, there was always room on the bench for them to sit silently by their father's side.

He constantly urged them to study hard. Mostly self-educated, Marshall made sure his sons attended college. Later, he encouraged his grandchildren to pay attention to their schoolwork. In a letter to one grandson, Marshall wrote, "Every man ought to be intimately acquainted with the history of his own country," and then, "There is no exercise of the mind from which more valuable improvement is to be drawn than from composition."[21] His concern with education extended beyond his immediate family. Unlike many Southerners of his day, Marshall wanted every child to receive a public education. This would teach them patriotism and make them good citizens.

Deeply in love with his wife, Marshall remained devoted to her throughout his life. When she was ailing, he would read aloud to her at night. He even did the family marketing. One day, when he was returning from the market with a basket of vegetables and some poultry, he met a man who had recently arrived in Richmond. The newcomer complained that he could get no one to deliver the turkey he had just purchased. Marshall took it home for him and refused payment for his services. As Marshall walked away, the man learned that his deliveryman was the Chief Justice of the United States.

Despite being mistaken for a deliveryman, John Marshall

This portrait of Polly Marshall, believed to have been done by her son Thomas Marshall around 1815, shows what she looked like at about fifty or sixty years of age.

still paid little attention to his appearances or his manners. On one occasion, when he was visiting friends for a meal, a young lady observed, "Judge Marshall was not a graceful man in society. He was abrupt and nervous in his movements and could not hand a lady a chair except most awkwardly with both hands, or a cup of tea without spilling it."[22] The Richmond ladies may have found him clumsy and ill at ease. Others, however, praised his treatment of women. Harriet Martineau, a famous crusader for women's rights, met Marshall. She wrote that he not only respected women but had "a steady conviction of their intellectual equality with men [and] a deep sense of their social injuries."[23] In those days, most men felt that women should depend on their fathers and husbands and accept their judgments and opinions without question. Unlike these men, Marshall accepted the fact that women had minds of their own.

Marshall took an active part in many of Richmond's social clubs. In addition to the Masons, he was a member of the Jockey Club, which organized horse races in May and October. He joined the Amicable Society, which gave refuge to stranded travelers and drifters who came to the state capital. He also belonged to the Society of the Cincinnati, an association of veterans of the Continental army. He was one of the first subscribers to the Richmond Circulating Library.

In 1788, he became a founding member of the Quoit Club, sometimes known as the Barbecue Club. For the next forty years, the members met on Saturdays for dinner and a game of quoits (pitching round flat disks made of stone or metal for distance and accuracy). Marshall had enjoyed playing quoits since childhood. Late in life, he was still intent on winning. A visitor to the club described an instance where an elderly Scottish gentleman was asked to decide between

Marshall's quoit and that of another gentleman. After carefully measuring the distances, he announced, " *Mister Marshall has it a leattle* ' when it was visible to all that the contrary was the case."[24]

John Marshall also enjoyed seeing the latest plays with his friends. In those days, audiences usually saw two different shows at one sitting. On December 26, 1811, the theater in Richmond burned down, filling the nearby Marshall home with smoke. Polly Marshall was frantic. Finally, she learned that her husband and their son John had not attended the performance but were busily fighting the fire. Many people they knew lost their lives in the burning theater. John Marshall was appointed to head a fund-raising committee to build a monument to the victims. So great was Marshall's love of plays that after his death, a new theater was named for him.

Not all of Marshall's activities with his friends were social. In 1816, he became one of the founders of the American Colonization Society. In 1823, this private charity set up a colony in Africa for free black farmers. The Society was very important in getting Congress to ban the slave trade. In 1827, Marshall served as president of the newly formed Virginia Society for Colonization. It relocated some of the forty thousand or so free blacks living in Virginia. Most had difficulty earning a living and nowhere to turn for help.[25]

Marshall was among those who favored a gradual end to slavery. In his will, he gave his slave, Robin, the chance to become a free man. Robin was offered $100 if he chose to go to Liberia, the colony for freed blacks in Africa, and $50 if he did not. If he did not want to be freed, he was to select one of the Marshall children as his owner and be provided with someone to care for him in his old age.[26] Robin chose freedom. The three other Marshall slaves refused freedom and chose instead to care for the Marshall grandchildren.

After nearly forty-nine years of marriage, Polly Marshall died on December 25, 1831, possibly from severe anemia, a blood disorder. Before her death, she placed the locket with her hair around her husband's neck. He wrote: "From the moment of our union to that of our separation, I never ceased to thank Heaven for this its best gift. Not a moment passed in which I did not consider her as a blessing from which the chief happiness of my life was derived."[27] He was to live without her for only four years. On July 6, 1835, the seventy-nine-year-old Chief Justice, weakened by a stagecoach accident, would die of liver disease, still wearing her locket.

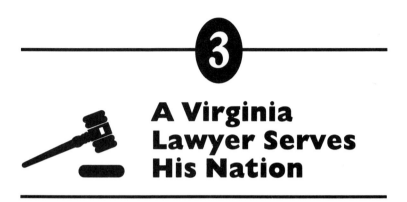

3

A Virginia Lawyer Serves His Nation

If John Marshall had never become Chief Justice of the Supreme Court, he still would have had an impressive career. Starting out as a lawyer, he first took part in state politics, then in national affairs. Marshall watched the American republic experiment with a weak central government under the Articles of Confederation. Then he saw a stronger national government develop under the Constitution. He also saw the nation's leaders arguing over the direction the new country should take. Their rivalry led to the rise of political parties.

As a young lawyer in Richmond, John Marshall mostly handled claims for veterans of the War of Independence. He helped them get pensions from Virginia and land promised by Congress as a reward for their military service. "They knew that I felt their wrongs and sympathized in their sufferings . . ."[1]

He quickly developed a reputation as a skilled attorney. Usually, he would analyze a case for its strengths and weaknesses. Then he would present one strong logical argument in support of his client. He had the gift of making both lawyers and nonlawyers understand his reasoning.

One time, a visiting country gentleman asked for an attorney. Marshall was pointed out as he strolled down the street. His shirt was hanging out of his knee breeches, and he was eating cherries out of his straw hat. Disappointed at Marshall's unprofessional appearance, the gentleman immediately hired another lawyer. This attorney wore a black suit and powdered wig. While waiting in court for his case to be tried, the gentleman watched Marshall and the other lawyer at work. Marshall was clearly superior. So the gentleman promptly introduced himself and asked Marshall to take his case. He confessed that he had mistaken legal clothing for legal skill. He also explained that he could only pay Marshall five dollars, all the money he had left. The other lawyer had charged him ninety-five dollars and would not return the fee. Marshall agreed to take the case and won it.

Despite his casual, sometimes sloppy, appearance, Marshall became a very successful lawyer. In the 1780s, he helped George Washington with a land claim, Thomas Jefferson with his late father-in-law's debts, and James Monroe with some unpaid bills. In 1786, he lost an important land case, *Hite* v. *Fairfax.* He did, however, convince the court to turn over the late Lord Fairfax's estates to a group of men, including himself.

To raise $20,000 (about $170,000 today) for his share of the Fairfax lands (some 160,000 acres), Marshall had to continue his profitable law practice. He also wanted to make sure that his wife's and children's future was secure.[2] As a result, he refused several offers to serve in the United States government. The pay was too low. In one instance in 1794, he wrote to President George Washington that he could not join the cabinet as attorney general. "The business I have undertaken to complete in Richmond forbids me to change my situation though for one infinitely more eligible."[3] Between 1790 and 1799, he argued 113 cases before the Virginia Court of Appeals.[4] By that time, he was earning about $5,000 a year from his law practice. This would be about $42,350 today.[5]

Marshall argued only one case before the Supreme Court, *Ware* v. *Hylton* (1796). He represented Virginians who refused to pay their debts to British creditors. Marshall claimed that his clients no longer owed any money to the British. During the war, the Virginia government had allowed its citizens to pay off these debts by contributing to a state fund. The opposing lawyer argued that the 1783 peace treaty with Britain, ending the War of Independence, required American citizens to pay the debts. Marshall, however, insisted that his clients were not bound by the treaty. It had not existed when Virginia canceled the debt.

Marshall was defending a position he personally opposed. He firmly believed that when federal law (the treaty) and state law (canceling the debts) conflicted, federal law was supreme.[6] Despite his personal conviction, he presented a convincing case for his clients. One observer wrote: "Marshall, it was acknowledged on all hands, excelled himself in *sound sense* and *argument*, which you know is saying an immensity."[7] Nevertheless, he lost the case.

In 1782, Marshall was elected a state lawmaker for the first time. He represented Fauquier County. He was soon made a councillor of state, a post previously held by his father and his father-in-law. (The council of state was a group of eight men who advised the governor on his programs and appointments to state offices.) Marshall was only twenty-seven years old at the time. A number of judges objected to someone so young holding the post. In 1784, they ruled that a councillor could not also be an active lawyer. Marshall, like many other state lawmakers, had continued to work as an attorney. Rather than give up his legal career with its profitable fees, he resigned from the council. During his first term in state government, he complained to James Monroe about his experiences. "Not a bill of public importance, in which an individual was not particularly interested has passed."[8] He did not run for reelection in 1785–1786, but he served again in 1787.

Marshall worried about the future of the new republic. In 1786, Massachusetts farmers, led by Daniel Shays, rebelled against a state law requiring them to pay their debts in cash. Under the Articles of Confederation, the weak national government was unable to raise an army to put down Shays' Rebellion. Marshall wrote: "I fear, and there is no opinion more degrading to the dignity of man, that those have truth on their side who say that man is incapable of governing himself."[9] Marshall, the nationalist, championed a stronger federal government with the resources to put down local rebellions. He was soon given the chance to explain his ideas.

In June 1788, John Marshall was one of the 168 Virginia delegates chosen to consider if Virginia should ratify (approve) the new Constitution of the United States. They met in Richmond for three weeks. Nine states had already ratified the document. This was the number necessary for the Constitution to go into effect. Because news traveled so slowly, the Virginians, however, did not know that theirs was no longer the deciding ninth vote. Marshall wrote an amusing verse describing the proceedings. It began:

The State's determined Resolution
Was to discuss the Constitution
For this members came together
Melting with zeal and sultry weather[10]

Despite abundant sunlight, the prospects for ratification were not very bright. Virginians had prospered under the Articles. They were reluctant to accept a new government system. One delegate to the convention thought that at least 80 percent of the population of Virginia did not want the new Constitution.[11] Their spokesmen included Patrick Henry, the first governor of Virginia; James Monroe, future president of the United States; and George Mason, a delegate to the 1787 Constitutional Convention in Philadelphia. Defending the Constitution were James Madison, a founder of the new government and future president; Chancellor George Wythe; and John Marshall, among others.

With his dry voice, thirty-four-year-old John Marshall could not hope to compete with such an accomplished public speaker as Patrick Henry. Marshall's casual clothes certainly failed to impress the elegantly dressed plantation owners. Few, however, could match his powers of reasoning. Marshall responded to criticisms that the Constitution made the Congress and the president too powerful. He argued that the House of Representatives would not abuse its powers, especially the power to tax. The House was elected by the people. Its members could also be turned out of office by the people. Marshall went on to defend the president's power to call up an army. The states could not be counted on to volunteer the troops and supplies that were needed. Perhaps, he had Shays' rebellion in mind when he spoke. He reminded the delegates that under the new system, the states still kept their own militias.

Marshall also answered the charge that federal courts were unnecessary. He insisted that independent federal courts were necessary to handle lawsuits between states and between citizens of different states. In his speech on the courts, he anticipated a landmark decision he would make as Chief Justice, fifteen years later. "To what quarter will you look for protection from an infringement on [violation of] the Constitution if you do not give the power to the judiciary? There is no other body which can afford such protection."[12]

Unlike the Constitution's opponents, Marshall welcomed a stronger national government. He stated, "I think the virtue and talents of the members of the general government will tend to the security, instead of the destruction, of our liberty."[13] The Virginia convention approved the Constitution by a vote of 89 to 79. Marshall's speeches had made an important contribution to the ratification process. They also brought him the admiration and respect of many of Virginia's leaders.

During the 1790s, two political parties, the Republicans and the Federalists, began to disagree over a number of government measures. One of their disagreements concerned the way the United States should treat France. The Revolution of 1789 had overthrown the French monarchy. Then the new French republic had gone to war with Great Britain and other European nations. Vice President Thomas Jefferson's Republicans urged the government to actively support the French military effort. To them, the French were fighting for liberty and democracy. President George

Washington's Federalists did not want the nation to become involved in foreign wars. They wanted the United States to be able to trade with both France and its enemies.

Like other Federalists, Marshall had quickly become disillusioned by the French Revolution. The new government of France had engaged in widespread massacres of its own citizens. One opponent of the government was the Marquis de Lafayette, Marshall's former commander during the War of Independence. He had fought in the French Revolution but opposed the continued violence. He had been forced to leave the country in 1792. Marshall deplored the way the French revolutionaries had treated the marquis.[14] Later, in 1824, the marquis paid a visit to Virginia. John Marshall was one of his hosts and gave many speeches praising the French leader's love of liberty and his service to America.

In 1793, President Washington issued the Proclamation of Neutrality. It kept Americans from taking sides in the European war. Upon his arrival in the United States, French diplomat Edmont Genet asked the American people to defy the Proclamation. He urged them to raise troops and outfit privateers, privately owned, armed vessels, officially licensed to attack enemy shipping, to go after the British. In 1794, Marshall had the chance to show what he thought of Genet's unprofessional behavior. He was sent to prevent an American ship, the *Unicorn*, from being converted to a French privateer. As a brigadier general in the Virginia militia, he led a small army to Smithfield, Virginia, the *Unicorn*'s port. Local opposition to the Proclamation of Neutrality was very strong. Marshall's show of force, however, was successful. He seized the ship's supply of arms without bloodshed.

John Marshall was one of the few Federalist lawmakers in Virginia. During the 1780s and '90s, he was reelected to the state government several times. He could no longer complain that nothing important was being accomplished. He forcefully defended the actions of President Washington's government. For example, in 1795, Marshall supported the Jay Treaty of 1794. The treaty contained British promises to give up its Northwest trading posts and open some ports in the West Indies to American traders. The United States consented to have American debts repaid to the British. The two nations agreed to settle future disputes peacefully. Despite Marshall's spirited defense of this Federalist achievement, the Virginia lawmakers officially condemned it by a vote of almost two to one.[15] Most of them were members of Jefferson's Republican party. They feared that the treaty would anger France.

In 1796, the French began to attack American shipping, to prevent cargoes from reaching Britain. Then the French government asked the American minister Charles Cotesworth Pinckney to leave the country or face arrest. In May 1797, President John Adams reported this latest French insult to Congress. To avoid a war, he offered to negotiate American differences with France.[16] President Adams asked Marshall to become part of a three-man diplomatic mission to France. The other members were Elbridge Gerry, a Republican from the North, and ousted minister Pinckney, a Federalist from the deep South.

Marshall did not speak French and lacked diplomatic experience. Nevertheless, he felt he could help in the negotiations.[17] Also, he would receive approximately $20,000. This sum would enable him make an additional payment on the Fairfax lands.[18] Marshall needed the extra money because he had taken over the shares of one of his partners who was bankrupt. Marshall expected to return to his law practice in six or seven months. Instead, he would spend more than thirteen months abroad.[19]

Before departing for Europe, the three men traveled to Philadelphia, then the nation's capital. There Secretary of State Timothy Pickering gave them detailed instructions about dealing with the French. They needed these guidelines before they left because letters shipped between the United States and France took months to arrive. The three men were told not to agree to aid France's war against Britain, not to sacrifice American trade anywhere in the world, and not to let their country be blamed for the difficulties between France and the United States.[20]

When the Americans arrived in Paris, the French government refused to treat them properly as diplomats. They were repeatedly denied an appointment to see the foreign minister, Talleyrand. Instead, he sent his unofficial agents, Hottenguer, Bellamy, and Hauteval, to deal with them. The agents tried to frighten the Americans with reports of continued American shipping losses at the hands of French privateers. The Frenchmen insisted that no negotiations could take place until three conditions were met. 1) President Adams had to apologize for his unkind remarks about France to Congress. 2) He had to promise France a $12 million loan. 3) The French agents had to receive a $25,000 bribe to guarantee a meeting with Talleyrand.

The diplomats found these demands unacceptable. Marshall wrote in his dispatches: "We could not easily believe that even our money would save us; our independence would never cease to give offense and would always furnish a pretext for fresh demands."[21] If they gave in, other nations would be tempted to blackmail the United States by attacking American ships to get American loans.

The three diplomats waited endlessly for Talleyrand to see them. Under pressure, they began to disagree among themselves. Republican Gerry favored any measure that would prevent war with France. Marshall and Pinckney refused to go along with him. The French tried to isolate Marshall and Pinckney. They preferred to deal with Gerry who appeared to be more sympathetic to their cause.

Nevertheless, Talleyrand's agents arranged for Pierre de Beaumarchais to appeal directly to Marshall. Beaumarchais had written the words for the operas *The Marriage of Figaro* and *The Barber of Seville*. Earlier, he had hired Marshall as his lawyer. The Frenchman was suing the state of Virginia for payment of war supplies he had sent to America during the War of Independence. He offered to pay Talleyrand's bribe with the money he might win in the lawsuit. Bribery of government officials was an accepted custom in France, but Marshall objected to it. He rejected Beaumarchais's plan.

Marshall wrote about his many frustrations in letters to his wife, his friends, and government officials. He told Polly how much he missed her. "Let me see you once more and I can venture to assert that no consideration can induce me ever again to consent to place the Atlantic between us."[22] He confided to Washington, "The Atlantic only can save us, and that no consideration will be sufficiently powerful to check the extremities to which the temper of this government will carry it, but an apprehension that we may be thrown into the arms of Britain."[23] In his dispatches to Pickering, he wrote, "My own private opinion is that this haughty ambitious government . . . will not condescend to act with justice or to treat us as a free & independent nation."[24]

President Adams reported on the dispatches to Congress. He deliberately left out the names of the French agents. Fearing

In the first page of a letter John Marshall wrote to his wife from France in 1797, he speaks of his disappointment at not having received any letters from the United States. Since the paper Marshall used was very thin, the other side of the letter shows through.

for the lives of his diplomats, he substituted the initials X, Y, and Z.[25] This is why the mission to France has been known to history as the XYZ affair. When the dispatches were made public, the American people's sympathy for France quickly turned to anger.

The American diplomats stayed on in Paris, despite the official insults they had received. They hoped that they still might settle the difficulties with France. Marshall drafted a lengthy letter to the French government. It reviewed American-French relations and repeated the American government's offer to negotiate its differences with France. Talleyrand never read the letter because it was too long. He did see the diplomats three times but refused to treat them as official representatives of their government. The meetings did not produce any results.

The Americans decided to go home. A disappointed Marshall wrote: "We regret the impossibility of consulting our government or those in whom we can confide. We must act upon our own judgments and our opinion is that we ought not remain much longer."[26] As a further insult, the French government delayed giving them the diplomatic passports they needed to return to the United States. Finally, Pinckney and Marshall were allowed to leave France, but Pinckney stayed on because his daughter was sick and unable to travel. Gerry remained in Paris waiting for new instructions from President Adams.

Marshall landed in New York on June 17, 1798, and proceeded directly to Philadelphia. He did not know whether he would be welcomed. The mission was not a success because the diplomats had not settled the dispute with France. On the other hand, they had shown that the United States could not be pushed around by a European power. As it

Marshall brought this clock back with him from his trip to France. The clock is still on display and can be seen by visitors at the John Marshall house in Richmond, Virginia.

turned out, Marshall was treated as a national hero. He was greeted by cheering crowds, invited to dinners and receptions by members of the government, and praised for not giving in under pressure. On June 23, the night before Marshall left for Richmond, he was honored with a now famous toast: "Millions for defense but not a cent for tribute."[27]

Upon his return to Virginia, Marshall was asked to run for Congress in the election of 1798. As a hero of the XYZ affair, he was the only Federalist who could possibly defeat the popular Republican candidate John Clopton. George Washington invited Marshall to Mount Vernon to convince him to become a candidate. Washington's nephew Bushrod accompanied Marshall. On the way there, the two men accidentally picked up saddle bags belonging to some other travelers. They appeared before the former president in ill-fitting clothes. Washington was very amused by the incident. Marshall proved to be a reluctant candidate. He wanted to return to his much neglected legal work. Washington, however, persuaded him to put the welfare of his country above his need to make money. Because of his love for the country and desire to strengthen the national government, Marshall gave in. This meant that he also had to turn down President Adams's offer to become a Justice of the Supreme Court. Bushrod Washington accepted the Justice position instead.

During his congressional campaign, Marshall received support from Patrick Henry, a member of Jefferson's political party. "Tell Marshall I love him because he felt and acted as a republican, as an American," Henry wrote.[28] In a series of letters to the voters, Marshall boldly condemned the Alien and Sedition Acts of 1798. Under these laws, the Federalist Congress had made it a crime to criticize the president of the

John Marshall's saddle bag, shown here, held his clothing and other possessions when he travelled.

United States. The Acts had already resulted in the arrest of many Jeffersonian editors, writers, and party members. It took courage for Marshall to speak out against the laws. He could not, however, support his party in violation of his nationalist principles. In his words, the Federalist laws would only "create unnecessary discontents and jealousies at a time when our very existence as a nation may depend on our union."[29]

On the other hand, Marshall opposed the way Republican state lawmakers in Kentucky and Virginia challenged these laws. In 1798 they declared that the Alien and Sedition Acts violated the Constitution and refused to obey them. More importantly, the lawmakers encouraged other states to follow their lead. In a letter to George Washington, Marshall objected to these Virginia and Kentucky Resolutions. He also criticized the politicians who voted for them. They had put the needs of their party before the needs of their country.

> Had they [the Alien and Sedition Laws] never been passed, other measures would have been selected. . . . Sentiments were declared and . . . views were developed of a very serious and alarming extent . . . These are men who will hold power by any means rather than not hold it; and who would prefer a dissolution of the union to a continuance of an administration not of their own party.[30]

Marshall won the election by only 108 votes. When the Sixth Congress met in 1799, it soon became his sad duty to announce the death of George Washington. "Our Washington is no more! The Hero, the Sage, and the Patriot of America—the man on whom in times of danger every eye was turned and all hopes were placed—lives now only in his own great actions and in the hearts of an affectionate and afflicted people."[31]

Marshall never forgot that he was a Federalist. Nevertheless, he showed his independence of party politics once more. He voted with the Republicans to cancel the Alien and Sedition Acts. The move failed, and the laws remained in force until 1801. As a congressman, he also helped write the first National Bankruptcy Act. This law helped free one of Marshall's partners in the Fairfax land purchase who had been imprisoned because he could not pay his bills.

Marshall defended Federalist President John Adams from Republican attacks in Congress. The Republicans were outraged when the president turned over sailor Jonathan Robbins to the British to be hanged for murder. The sailor, a British subject, claimed American citizenship. The Republicans supported his plea to be tried in an American court. Marshall quickly disproved their arguments. He explained why an American court could not hear the case. Under Article 27 of the Jay Treaty, Britain and the United States had pledged to return each other's fugitives from justice. Marshall reasoned that the Constitution gave the president responsibility for foreign policy. The Robbins affair was a foreign policy matter, not a judicial one. Even if Robbins had been an American citizen, he would not have been entitled to a trial in American courts. At the conclusion of Marshall's speech, Republican Congressman Albert Gallatin was supposed to criticize the Federalist position. He was so impressed by Marshall's reasoning that he could not argue with him. He stood up and explained, "There is absolutely no reply to make, for his speech is unanswerable."[32]

On May 12, 1800, two days before Congress went home, President Adams named Marshall as his secretary of state without consulting him. The surprised congressman wrote: "I never felt more doubt than on the question of accepting or declining this offer. I could not bring myself to yield to it. On the other hand, the office was precisely that which I wished, and for which I had vanity enough to think myself fitted."[33] He accepted the position and received a salary of $5,000.[34] His duties included corresponding with American diplomats abroad and with European governments. Occasionally, he met with foreign diplomats in the United States. Despite the demands of his job, he still had time to go to Richmond to argue a lawsuit.

In 1801, Marshall turned down a request from Alexander Hamilton, the nation's first secretary of the Treasury and a leading Federalist. Hamilton wanted Marshall's help to elect Thomas Jefferson president. In the election of 1800, two Republicans, Thomas Jefferson and Aaron Burr, had received the same number of votes. Because of the tie, the House of Representatives had to choose the next president. Hamilton managed to convince Marshall that Burr was a dangerous man. Marshall, however, could not overcome his fear that Jefferson would "sap the fundamental principles of the government."[35] So the secretary of state refused to use his influence to win votes for Jefferson and remained on the sidelines. The House elected Jefferson anyway. Seven years later, Chief Justice Marshall would have another opportunity to decide between Jefferson and Burr.

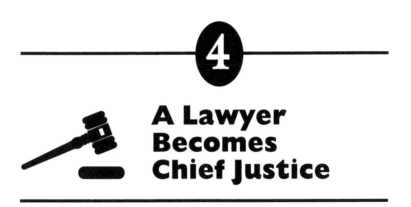

A Lawyer Becomes Chief Justice

John Marshall served on the Supreme Court for thirty-four years, a record matched by only two other Justices and broken by a third. The procedures and practices Marshall introduced made the Court a powerful branch of the government. The decisions he made helped to shape the future of American laws. Yet, he was not President Adams's first choice for Chief Justice.

In December 1800, the nation's third Chief Justice of the Supreme Court, Oliver Ellsworth, resigned due to illness. Defeated president John Adams was determined to replace him with another Federalist to keep his party in control of the courts. A Republican president and Congress would soon take office. Adams reviewed his possible choices. Associate Justice William Cushing was too old to be Chief Justice. The appointment of younger William Paterson would probably offend the senior Justice. So Adams asked former Chief Justice John Jay to return to the post. Jay turned him down because he said the Court lacked "the public confidence and respect."[1]

On January 19, 1801, President Adams turned to his forty-five-year-old Secretary of State John Marshall. Marshall was personally loyal to him, logical in his reasoning, and an excellent leader. The president said, "I believe I must nominate you," and Marshall replied that he was "pleased as well as surprized[sic]."[2] The next day, Adams asked the Senate for approval, as the Constitution required. The Senate held up the vote for a week, hoping that Adams would change his mind in favor of Paterson. As a Federalist, Marshall was too unpredictable and independent. He had even opposed the party's Alien and Sedition laws.

The president stood firm. On January 27, Marshall became the new Chief Justice by a unanimous vote. At Adams's request, he also stayed on as secretary of state for the rest of the president's term in office. He received a yearly salary of $4,000 (equal to about $33,880 today).[3] Associate Justices were paid $3,500 (equal to about $29,645 today). In 1819, his salary was increased to $5,000 (equal to about $42,350 today). For comparison, in 1993 the Chief Justice was paid $171,500 a year and an Associate Justice, $164,100.[4]

Over the years, the Supreme Court had been sadly neglected. On the day Adams chose Marshall, the District Commissioners wrote to Congress. "As no house has been provided for the Judiciary of the United States, we hope the Supreme Court may be accommodated with a room in the Capitol to hold its sessions until further provision shall be made."[5] The Justices met in a Senate committee room on the main floor of the Capitol for seven years. Then, they were moved to the basement below the Senate chamber. The new location was so small that the Justices had to put on their robes in front of the spectators. In 1818, the courtroom was remodeled. The Justices were seated on a raised platform at the east end of the room. Onlookers occupied a double row of chairs or stood among the many arches which held up the Senate chamber floor.

When Marshall took office, the reputation of the Court was as disappointing as its surroundings. Chief Justices had been busy with nonlegal matters. Chief Justice John Jay was sent to Britain to negotiate a treaty in 1794. The following year, he won election for governor of New York while he was still a member of the Court. From 1799 to 1800 Chief Justice Oliver Ellsworth served on a special diplomatic mission to France that was unrelated to his official duties.

John Marshall began a Supreme Court tradition by discouraging the Justices from getting involved in politics. He set an example by declining to vote in national elections. He was very angry when a newspaper reported that he would vote in the 1828 presidential elections. He promptly wrote a reply, denying the story. He did not mind if the public learned about his private opinions of the candidates. (In that election, he favored John Quincy Adams over Andrew Jackson.) What really upset him was that the newspaper article made him look like a hotheaded politician rather than a thoughtful judge.[6]

Marshall also changed court procedures. Before he took charge, each Justice presented his own opinion (judgment) of a case, as was done in England. Marshall convinced the Justices to unite as a majority behind a single opinion. This let the Court speak with one voice and gave its decisions more weight. Those who disagreed with the majority's judgment, however, could write dissenting opinions. Since Marshall's time, the Supreme Court has continued to present its decisions this way.

For meetings of the Court, the six Justices came to Washington, D.C., now the nation's capital, without their families. (After 1807, there were seven members of the Court. Congress fixed the number at nine in 1869 after a series of increases and decreases in the 1830s and 1860s.) They all lived in the same boarding house. It became their home and their office. They ate meals together and discussed the cases they had to decide. These arrangements helped them develop a common outlook.

John Marshall was a natural leader. With tact and firmness, he could get the other Justices to support his judgments. His sense of humor and colorful anecdotes kept their spirits high. Justice Joseph Story wrote: "I love his laugh, it is too hearty for an intriguer, and his good temper and unwearied patience are equally agreeable on the bench and in the study."[7] The Justices enjoyed the story of how Marshall was challenged to a word game during a brief visit to a men's club in Philadelphia. He had to make up a poem describing the word paradox, which is a statement that seems to contradict itself but is true. He recited:

> In the bluegrass regions of Kentucky
> A paradox was born
> The corn was full of kernels
> And the colonels full of corn[8]

One time, a young lawyer complimented him on his judicial distinction and ability. He replied, "Let me tell you what that means, young man. The acme of judicial distinction means the ability to look a lawyer straight in the eyes for two hours and not hear a damned word he says."[9]

As Chief Justice, Marshall read the oath of office to incoming presidents. He swore in Thomas Jefferson, James Madison, James Monroe, John Quincy Adams, and Andrew Jackson. He was very uneasy when presidents Jefferson and Jackson took office. He objected to their views of democracy. They encouraged ordinary citizens to take part in politics. They also relied on political parties to convince the public to be on their side.

Marshall did not want to see the common people take power and was upset when political parties actively competed for their votes.[10] Parties appealed to people's feelings rather than their thoughts. They made the public lose sight of what was good for the nation as a whole. Instead of taking power themselves, the people should elect the best leaders possible to make decisions for them. The leaders could always be voted out of office if they used their power to hurt the public. These were views Marshall held throughout his life.

Marshall defended his views as late as 1829 when he was a member of the Virginia Convention to change the state constitution. Marshall convinced the Convention to continue to require citizens to own property in order to vote. That way they would vote more responsibly. They would think about their economic interests and be less likely to let their feelings control them. He did, however, agree that property qualification should be lowered.[11] This would allow more people to take part in elections.

In 1830, he wrote a letter to a friend suggesting that the method of electing presidents be changed. "The passions of men are influenced to so fearful an extent, large masses are so embittered against each other, that I dread the consequences."[12] He suggested that the people choose a number of candidates. The president would be chosen from among them by lot.[13] His idea was never taken seriously.

Until 1891, members of the Supreme Court also served as federal circuit court judges. If a circuit court case came to the Supreme Court, the Justice in charge of that circuit might have to decide the same case twice. To avoid this, individual Justices disqualified themselves. Marshall was assigned to the fifth circuit in Virginia and North Carolina to hear appeals from federal courts. He traveled to Richmond, Virginia, in May and November and to North Carolina, in June and December and held court. He spent only six to ten weeks a year on the Supreme Court in Washington, D.C.

In January 1803, he wrote to his wife about the difficulties he faced on the circuit. Besides bumpy roads that made traveling uncomfortable, he once complained that he had had to wear trousers in court. It was customary for the judges to wear knee breeches. Unfortunately, Marshall's servant had forgotten to pack the breeches, and no tailor in Raleigh had time to make him a new pair. To add to his woes, he had lost fifteen silver dollars through a hole in his much mended waistcoat [vest] pocket.[14]

In 1807, John Marshall conducted the trial of Jefferson's former vice president, Aaron Burr, in Richmond. He was assisted by District [trial] Judge Cyrus Griffin. The ordeal took seven months and involved more than 140 witnesses. Burr, a puzzling figure in American history, was accused of treason. He was charged with leading a conspiracy to seize western lands and attack Mexico to build an empire. Marshall, the nationalist, could not admire a man charged with trying to take territory away from the United States. Nor could he respect the man who had killed Alexander Hamilton in a duel.[15]

CHIEF JUSTICE MARSHALL.

This cartoon pokes fun at John Marshall's sloppy appearance during one of his trips to Richmond, Virginia, as a circuit court judge. He is shown wearing torn knee breeches while talking to a group of well-dressed young lawyers in a Virginia tavern.

President Jefferson had his own grudges against Burr and declared him guilty before the trial was even held. His statements inflamed the already panicky public. Under these circumstances, Marshall was especially determined that Burr be treated fairly. More than once, he had to warn the lawyers against trying Burr "by artificially excited public opinion instead of by law and evidence."[16] Getting a jury was difficult. Too many people had already made up their minds that Burr was guilty. Drawn from Richmond citizens, many of the jurors were friends or relatives of the Marshall or the Jefferson families. Marshall had to instruct them to enter the trial "with minds open to those impressions, which the testimony and the law of the case ought to make" and not with popular prejudices in mind.[17]

Marshall's own impartiality was also questioned. He set off a furor by ruling that Burr could be released on bail. (Bail is money deposited with the court to insure that a person will appear for trial.) After hearing lawyers for both sides, Marshall decided there wasn't enough evidence of treason to keep Burr in custody. Only after the grand jury brought charges against Burr, was he imprisoned. The Richmond City Jail was said to be unhealthy. So Burr was given some rooms in a penitentiary just outside the city. There he was allowed to receive visitors.

Marshall soon upset the public again. He dined at the home of his friend, John Wickham, Burr's chief lawyer. He had not known that Burr would also be a guest. Marshall did not talk with Burr during the meal and left soon afterward. Whether he was wise to remain once Burr appeared is debatable. He certainly gave Burr's enemies reason to think he favored Burr.

Marshall caused another uproar. He ordered President Jefferson to turn over certain papers Burr needed for his

The trial of Aaron Burr was a difficult one. Too many people had already made up their minds that Burr was guilty. The jury was drawn from Richmond citizens and many were friends or relatives of the Marshall or Jefferson families.

defense. Marshall stated that "the uniform practice of this country has been to permit any individual, who was charged with any crime, to prepare for his defence, and to obtain the process of the court, for the purpose of enabling him to do so."[18] The president was reluctant to obey the order. If courts began issuing such orders to him, he would have little time left for governing the nation.[19] Eventually, Jefferson did send the needed papers to Richmond. He did not seem to care whether Burr had a fair trial, but Marshall did. He gave the defense every opportunity to be heard.

The Constitution makes it difficult to get convictions for treason. The nation's founders wanted to protect innocent citizens from unduly suspicious government officials. They did, however, want the government to be able to punish its real enemies. This is why the Constitution requires two witnesses to testify in a treason trial. They must swear to have seen an act of war committed against the United States. They must also be able to identify the person who committed the act. Marshall reviewed these constitutional requirements with the jury.

None of the witnesses at Burr's trial actually saw him commit treason.[20] They could only prove that some sort of a secret plot existed. Armed men had assembled on an island, departed by flatboats for New Orleans, and met Burr near Natchez, Mississippi. Burr had written a sketchy letter about his plans, but no one will ever know with certainty what he intended to do. Since he did not carry out his vague plans, the jury acquitted him. The public was furious. So was President Thomas Jefferson.

By holding to the precise words of the Constitution, Marshall had made the action (betraying the country) more important than the intention (the plot). Marshall's ruling on treason was very unpopular at the time. Nevertheless, it lasted until the First World War. Even then, Congress specifically called secret plots to aid the nation's enemies "espionage," rather than "treason." This made it easier to get convictions.

Marshall's official duties left him with plenty of time for other activities. He accepted Associate Justice Bushrod Washington's offer to write a biography of George Washington. There were five volumes in all, published between 1804 and 1807. They were written to remind people of Washington's principles of good government, not to recount his character or personal life. In 1826, Marshall even prepared a shorter version for children to read. The Chief Justice's work on the biography helped him make decisions about the Constitution.[21] He read the writings of the nation's founders. He learned what they had hoped to accomplish. Some of these men were even his friends.

Marshall also accepted a post from the Virginia lawmakers. He led an expedition to survey rivers as possible sites for canals in the state's unsettled areas. Canals would make it easier for Virginians to trade with people living in Kentucky and Ohio. Having grown up in the backwoods, Marshall knew how to survive in the wilderness. He was traveling with the expedition when the War of 1812 broke out.

At Republican President James Madison's request, Congress declared war against Britain. British ships had been capturing American sailors and making them work as British seamen. As a result, American shipping was interrupted. Like other Federalists, Marshall opposed the war.[22] It would destroy profitable trading relations with Britain and possibly involve the United States in the ongoing struggle between France and Britain in Europe. Despite his objections to the

63

war, however, Marshall served on a vigilance committee appointed by the city council of Richmond from 1813–1814. The committee made preparations to protect the city from a possible British attack. The attack never came.

Of course, John Marshall is best remembered as a Chief Justice. His decisions became an important part of American history. For the most part, they were written in plain language. They contained few references to other law cases. The Supreme Court had only existed for about a decade and had not accomplished much. So Marshall could not look to its previous decisions for guidance. Instead, he relied on the words found in the Constitution.

The Constitution contained general ideas as well as specific rules. Marshall explained what the words in the document meant and applied them to legal disputes. Through his interpretations of the Constitution, he protected the rights of property owners, promoted the growth of the national government, and encouraged the expansion of trade and commerce (business). Not everyone agreed with his reasoning or his rulings. Some people wanted state governments to remain as powerful as they had been under the Articles of Confederation.

Marshall protected property owners from state governments' attempts to take away their land or limit the ways it could be used. For example, in 1810, he ruled that newly elected lawmakers in Georgia could not take back land that earlier corrupt state lawmakers had already given to property owners.[23] According to Marshall, once its lawmakers had sold the land, a state could not cancel the deal. Marshall reasoned that the sale of land was a contract, an agreement to do or not do something. Article I, Section 10 of the Constitution specifically prevented states from breaking or changing contracts. As a result of Marshall's decision, state governments were limited in their power to change existing rules about private property. In effect, those who bought lands from the state could keep them. This even included speculators, people who buy and sell property for profit.

Using similar reasoning, John Marshall also protected Dartmouth College from changes imposed by New Hampshire lawmakers in 1819.[24] Dartmouth President John Wheelock had been dismissed after many disputes with the trustees, the governing board of the college. He then asked the lawmakers to turn the private college into a public university. The state appointed new university officials to replace the college's trustees. The trustees refused to accept them. Despite the trustees' opposition, the new secretary-treasurer, William H. Woodward, took charge of the college records. When he refused to return them to the trustees, they sued him in court.

A royal charter, a legal document giving certain rights to a person or company, had created Dartmouth College as a private, nonprofit, corporation. The nation's founders may not have had royal charters in mind when they wrote the Constitution. Nevertheless, Marshall reasoned that the charter was a type of contract. The Constitution forbade states from changing agreements made by contract. This is why the Chief Justice ruled that the trustees could keep the college's property, contributions of land, and money. He held that the state had violated the Constitution and its own constitution by changing the charter.

Marshall's decision helped to protect private nonprofit corporations, such as colleges, from state controls. It also benefited business corporations which were beginning to form. It made their property secure from state interference.

The Court did allow, however, states to insert clauses into contracts, providing for future changes. They could also use their police powers (control over public health and safety) to issue rules affecting contracts.

In a famous 1824 steamboat case, *Gibbons* v. *Ogden*,[25] Marshall further strengthened the national government's control over the states. He defended Congress's power to make rules about commerce between states. He also extended this power to include trade within the borders of a state. The state of New York had given Robert Fulton and Robert Livingston a monopoly, the exclusive right to run steam boats in its waters. Then the two men sold Aaron Ogden the right to operate a ferry service between New York and New Jersey. Thomas Gibbons, however, started his own steamboat company to take passengers to and from the two states. Ogden went to court to stop him. Gibbons claimed that he had a federal coasting license that let him into any port he wished. The case eventually reached the Supreme Court.

Marshall decided in Gibbons's favor. As a nationalist, he could come to no other conclusion. He held that federal law (the coasting license) was supreme over state law (the monopoly). Admittedly, states had the right to supervise many types of trade through their police powers. When their actions conflicted with a federal law, however, they had to obey the federal law. Marshall also reminded Americans that trade wars among the states led to the writing of the Constitution. "The power over commerce, including navigation, was one of the primary objects for which the people of America adopted their government . . ."[26] He had extended the constitutional definition of commerce to include navigation within a state's waters. "Commerce among the states cannot stop at the external boundary line of each state, but may be introduced into the interior."[27]

This was a popular decision. By encouraging competition, it soon made steamboat fares less expensive. It also helped the nation's growing water transportation system. Southerners, however, were alarmed by Marshall's reasoning. They dreaded the prospect that Congress might use its powers over commerce to free slaves.

Less well known was Marshall's concern for the rights of oppressed minorities, such as African and Native Americans. He was ahead of his time and often offended public opinion. After he became Chief Justice, the nation increasingly divided over the issue of slavery. Most Southern politicians, like John C. Calhoun of South Carolina, defended slavery as the only economical way to grow cotton. On the other hand, Marshall continued to support the gradual release of slaves from servitude. In an 1826 letter, he wrote that "Nothing portends more calamity & mischief to the Southern States than their slave population. Yet they seem to cherish the evil . . ."[28] In 1831, Nat Turner's slave rebellion in Virginia resulted in the deaths of sixty-one whites and struck fear into most Southerners. Yet John Marshall was proud when his son Tom, a Virginia lawmaker, gave a speech urging that slaves be set free.[29]

As Chief Justice, there was little Marshall could do to end slavery. The Constitution had made it legal. He did, however, speak to the conscience of the nation. For example, in an 1825 case, he condemned the slave trade as immoral.[30] An American ship had intercepted a Spanish-Portuguese slaver carrying 280 Africans. International law required that the slaves be returned to their owners. Marshall demanded proof of ownership before he would restore the Africans to their

There was little that the law allowed John Marshall to do about slavery in his capacity as Chief Justice of the Supreme Court. He could and did, however, speak to the conscience of the nation.

captors. For about 120 slaves, such proof could not be produced. They were freed and sent to Liberia. In an 1829 case, a slave owner sued a steamship company. His slaves had drowned in an accident. He wanted the company to pay him for his lost property. Marshall lectured that a slave was a human being, not personal property.[31]

Slavery was not the only issue dividing the North and South. The South had claimed the right to nullify, or reject, federal laws raising tariffs, which are government fees charged on goods made abroad and sold in the United States. Marshall applauded President Jackson's strong stand against nullification. Nevertheless, he was pessimistic about the future. In a letter written in 1832, he admitted, "I yield slowly and reluctantly to the conviction that our Constitution cannot last. . . . Our opinions [in the South] are incompatible with a united government even among ourselves. The union has been prolonged this far by miracles."[32] He doubted the Union would survive the differences between its sections.

Marshall also spoke out about the way government treated Native Americans. Georgia wanted Cherokee lands for cotton cultivation and extended its jurisdiction, or control, over the Native Americans. By the 1800s, the Cherokees were a peaceful farming people with their own constitution and laws. They appealed to the national government for protection, a right guaranteed by their treaties with the United States. In 1830 President Andrew Jackson responded with his Indian Removal Bill. It forced the Cherokees to be uprooted from their lands and moved to the West. Marshall expressed his opinion of this policy in a private letter. "Humanity must bewail the course which is pursued . . ."[33]

The Cherokees learned that the land set aside for them in Oklahoma territory was ill-suited to farming. In 1831 they sued Georgia in the Supreme Court,[34] claiming to be members of an independent nation. The Constitution gave nations the right to bring cases directly to the Supreme Court. Marshall ruled that the Cherokees were not a nation but wards of the United States. In other words, they were a dependent people, needing government protection and guidance. He reluctantly dismissed the case. Although his decision was sound law, Marshall may have regretted it. He asked Court publisher Richard Peters to devote a separate volume to the case and even apologized for the decision.[35]

Meanwhile, a Cherokee named Corn Tassels murdered another member of his tribe. He was tried by a Georgia court. His lawyer claimed that under a treaty with the national government, Corn Tassels could only be tried by his own people. The Georgia court ignored this argument and found him guilty. His lawyer appealed to the Supreme Court. Despite a ruling in Corn Tassel's favor,[36] defiant Georgia officials executed him.

Marshall took on the state of Georgia again in 1832.[37] Officials had imprisoned Vermont missionary Samuel Worcester. He had entered Cherokee land without a state permit. A Georgia court released him. As a postmaster for the Cherokees, Worcester was a national government employee, exempt from the need for a permit. He was, however, ordered to leave the state. When he refused, he was arrested again. He appealed to the Supreme Court.

Marshall ruled in Worcester's favor, saying:

> A weak state, in order to provide for its safety, may place itself under the protection of one more powerful, without stripping itself of the right of self-government, and ceasing to be a state. . . . The Cherokee Nation . . . is a distinct community . . . in

which the laws of Georgia can have no force, and
which the citizens of Georgia have no right to enter
but with the assent of the Cherokees themselves, or in
conformity with treaties, and with the acts of
Congress.[38]

In this opinion, Marshall restored dignity to the Cherokee
people. He was unable to do much more.

President Jackson was outraged by Marshall's decision. He
is said to have snapped, "Well, John Marshall has made his
decision; now let him enforce it."[39] Worcester remained in
jail, and in 1838 the Cherokees set out on their "Trail of
Tears" to the Oklahoma territory. In Marshall's decisions
about slaves and Indians, he could only appeal to the
conscience of the American public and their leaders. He did
not have the power to make them act as he desired. The
Supreme Court has no way of forcing people to obey its
rulings.

Despite these setbacks, Marshall continued his efforts to
educate the nation through his judicial opinions. Marshall
favored having Supreme Court decisions printed at
government expense.[40] To preserve and defend their liberty,
the people had to understand their rights under the law.
Marshall did his best to explain what those rights were. His
decisions are still read today.

A Chief Justice's Landmark Decisions

John Marshall's first constitutional case as Chief Justice, *Marbury* v. *Madison,* was a landmark decision. He came up with an ingenious solution that recognized Marbury's right to have his commission as a justice of the peace. On the other hand, it did not give President Jefferson and Secretary of State Madison the chance to defy the Supreme Court. More importantly, Marshall's decision made the Supreme Court a truly independent branch of government. It made judicial history.

At age forty-five, John Marshall was still gawky and awkward. According to one observer, "The Chief Justice of the United States is in his person tall, . . . his muscles so relaxed as . . . to destroy everything like harmony in his air and his movements."[1] John Marshall, however, managed to get the Court to act harmoniously, to approve his decision.

His task was made easier because only two other members of the Supreme Court had heard the case from beginning to end. They were Bushrod Washington and Samuel Chase. Bushrod Washington, a quiet, studious man, was willing to follow his friend Marshall's lead. Then there was "Bacon Face," Samuel Chase of Maryland, with his bright red complexion and white hair.[2] The Republican Congress was trying to remove him from the Court. He was unlikely to favor the Republican secretary of state, James Madison. Justice William Paterson, a former governor of New Jersey, missed the first day, and Justice Alfred Moore of North Carolina did not arrive until the last day of argument. They went along with the others. Absent was Justice Cushing, the only Justice to wear an elaborate wig like English judges did. He was ill.

On February 24, 1803, ten days after the case was heard, the Supreme Court announced its decision. For the first time in its brief history, the Court united behind a single opinion and spoke with one voice. The voice was Marshall's. It took Marshall an hour and a half to read the opinion that he wrote to the public. He used some of that time to lecture the president and the secretary of state on their duties under the law. He reminded them that the law applied to officials and citizens alike.[3] In the main part of his decision, the Chief Justice answered three basic questions. 1) Did Marbury have a right to demand his commission as a justice of the peace? 2) Could Marbury request a *writ of mandamus* to force Madison to deliver the commission? 3) Should the Supreme Court issue this order?[4]

Marshall's answers to the first two questions were routine and humdrum. First, Marbury was entitled to his commission. After all, his appointment had been approved by the Senate, the commission had been signed by the president

In 1803, for the first time in its history, the Supreme Court was united behind a single decision. That decision in the *Marbury* v. *Madison* case, delivered by Chief Justice John Marshall, established judicial review.

and sealed by the secretary of state. Of course, Marshall could have said that the commission had to be delivered for it to be valid. That, however, would not have suited his purposes. Instead, he insisted that "it is not necessary that the delivery should be made personally . . ."[5]

Second, Marbury could request a *writ of mandamus* to force Madison to carry out his legal duties. Marshall admitted that "Questions in their nature political . . . can never be made in this court."[6] The Court could not interfere with the president's political decisions. Then Marshall ruled that Marbury's commission was a legal question, not a political question. Madison had not performed one of his official duties. Congressional law required the secretary of state to attach the Great Seal of the United States to official documents and to record them. Madison could not produce a record of Marbury's commission. So the writ was the proper solution.

Whether Madison would obey the court order was another matter. Marshall, however, made sure that the problem of enforcement would never come up. He had deliberately reversed the usual order of questions. He discussed the third issue, the Court's right to hear the case, last instead of first. This gave him the chance he needed to do the unexpected. He questioned the jurisdiction of the Supreme Court to hear the case. In doing so, he made judicial history. He turned a minor case about a government job into a landmark decision.

In Section 13 of the Judiciary Act of 1789, Congress had given the Supreme Court original jurisdiction to issue *writs of mandamus*. Under original jurisdiction, the Supreme Court could act as a trial court. It could hear the case for the first time rather than wait for an appeal from a trial court.

Marshall, however, found Section 13 violated the Constitution. According to him, the Constitution gave the Court original jurisdiction only in cases involving "ambassadors, other public ministers and consuls, and those in which a state shall be a party."[7] He could have let Congress add to the Court's original jurisdiction but not subtract from it. However, it suited his purposes to limit the types of cases the Court could hear. As a result, he ruled that the Supreme Court could not issue the *writ of mandamus*. Marbury would have to go to a trial court to get it.

Marshall deliberately limited the Court's jurisdiction in order to expand its powers. His analysis of Section 13 led him to strike down an act of Congress. This was the first time the Supreme Court declared an act of Congress unconstitutional. In doing so, the Supreme Court had claimed the power of judicial review. Judicial review lets the Justices decide whether the actions of the other branches of the national government and the actions of state governments are allowed under the Constitution. It made the Court a truly independent and important branch of government. Marshall had already defended judicial review at the Virginia Convention of 1788. He had stated: "If they [the national government] were to make a law not warranted by any of the powers enumerated [listed], it would be considered by the judges as an infringement on [violation of] the Constitution which they are to guard. . . . They would declare it void."[8]

Marshall wanted the courts to decide if a law violated the Constitution. As Chief Justice, however, he had to overcome an important obstacle. The Constitution did not mention judicial review. In *Marbury* v. *Madison,* he could only say that the document "confirms and strengthens the principle."[9] He had already shown that the Constitution was superior to ordinary laws. Therefore, laws that violated the Constitution could not be enforced.[10] After all, the Constitution gave the courts the right to hear all cases arising under it, and judges took an oath to support the Constitution.[11]

There was little public reaction to Marshall's decision. Americans were more interested in President Jefferson's recent purchase of the Louisiana Territory from France.[12] They seemed to take judicial review for granted. After all, it was what the nation's founders as well as the authors of the *Federalist Papers* had expected the Supreme Court to do.[13] The *Federalist Papers* were a series of essays urging approval of the Constitution. *Federalist Paper #78*, written by Marshall's friend Alexander Hamilton, even anticipated Marshall's reasoning in *Marbury v. Madison.*[14] In 1802, Republican lawmakers, too, had expected judicial review to occur.[15] This may have been why they had postponed the next meeting of the Supreme Court until 1803. No one had questioned the Court's right to review state laws. Now, the Court had overturned an act of Congress, but the landmark case was more or less ignored.

Meanwhile, the Court went about its business. It took charge of interpreting the Constitution and deciding what its words meant. As Marshall had stated, "It is emphatically the . . . duty of the judicial department to say what the law is."[16] A growing nation would pass laws on a wide variety of subjects, not always included in the Constitution. As a result, the Justices would have to apply the Constitution to new developments and new situations. One such development was the creation of the Second Bank of the United States in 1816. The Bank managed the nation's supply of money, received funds paid to the government, and set limits on state and private bank loans. It was not a popular body. Its eighteen branch offices competed with state banks for customers. It was also blamed for the nation's economic downturn in 1819.

Banks were not specifically mentioned in the Constitution. As a result, in 1819, the Supreme Court was asked to make a decision about Congress's right to set up the Bank and a state's right to tax it. The case provided Marshall with another opportunity for a landmark decision. A number of states with branch offices of the Bank were interested in Marshall's decision.

In 1818, the state of Maryland had challenged the power of the Bank of the United States. It passed a law requiring bank notes to be issued on stamped paper sold by the state. Banks could refuse to buy the paper, but they would have to pay a penalty tax of $15,000 (about $112,000 today).[17] James W. McCulloch, a cashier in the Maryland branch of the Bank defied state officials. He refused to buy the stamped paper or pay the tax.

Despite his opposition to the Maryland law, McCulloch was not a hero. He had been helping the Bank's directors to cheat the national government. The directors "lent" themselves over a million dollars, never intending to repay the "loans." McCulloch falsified bank records to hide their activities. He did not lose his job or face charges for his part in this crime until May 1819.[18]

Meanwhile he was sued in Baltimore County Court for failing to pay the $15,000 tax. He lost the case. Then the Maryland Court of Appeals heard the case, and McCulloch lost again. He appealed to the Supreme Court to come to his rescue. John Marshall had owned shares in the Bank. He sold off his stock before the lawyers for each side presented their arguments. If he had no monetary interest in the Bank, he could give an impartial judgment. He would not have to disqualify himself from deciding this important case.

From February 22 to March 3, 1819, spectators packed the Court's basement room to hear the opposing lawyers present their arguments. Former congressman Daniel Webster, Attorney General William Wirt, and William Pinckney, a prominent Baltimore lawyer, spoke for the Bank. Elderly Luther Martin, a member of the Constitutional Convention of 1787, and two highly respected lawyers, Joseph Hopkinson and Walter Jones, represented the state of Maryland. The speeches for both sides were eloquent. Marshall even complimented them in his decision on *McCulloch* v. *Maryland*.[19] The lawyers had to answer two questions. 1) Did Congress have the power to set up a Bank? 2) Did Maryland have the right to tax the Bank?

In his opening arguments, Daniel Webster reviewed Alexander Hamilton's reasons for setting up the original National Bank in 1791. (The First National Bank existed until 1811.) Then he reminded his listeners that the nation had had a bank for many years. It was too late to deny Congress the power to set up another one.[20] According to Webster, the Bank was an organization created by the national government. By taxing the Bank, Maryland was actually taxing the national government itself. Then he used a phrase John Marshall later made famous in his opinion, the "power to tax involves . . . a power to destroy."[21] If an organization repeatedly had to pay increasing taxes, it would not have enough money left to continue to operate.

Speaking for Maryland, seventy-five-year-old Luther Martin showed why he was still a clever lawyer. He began by quoting John Marshall's speeches from the Virginia Convention of 1788. During those debates over the

Constitution, Marshall had emphasized that the federal government would have limited powers.[22] Luther then described the limits set by the Tenth Amendment to the Constitution.[23] It reserved to the states all powers not specifically given by the Constitution to the national government. The power to set up a bank was not mentioned in the Constitution. Therefore it must be reserved to the states. When Congress created the Bank, it had abused its power.

Next it was William Pinckney's turn to argue before the Court. For three days, he spoke passionately in defense of the Bank. His sparkling phrases, precise reasoning, and brilliant arguments won the admiration of the Justices and crowds. It was perhaps the greatest speech of his life, and certainly one of the longest. It made an enormous impact on John Marshall. In planning and preparing his decision, he used much of what Pinckney had said.[24]

Meanwhile, starting on February 18, Congress began to debate the fate of the Bank. A member of the House of Representatives proposed a law to end the Bank's existence. The debate went on for five days, but the measure was defeated. It would be up to the Supreme Court to determine the Bank's future.

Marshall led members of the Court in private discussions of the case. One observer described him as "a man who is tall to awkwardness, with a large head of hair, which looked as if it had not been lately tied or combed, and with dirty boots."[25] Sixteen years had passed since *Marbury* v. *Madison.* Marshall's looks had not improved, but his leadership of the Court had become even stronger.

He managed to get all the Justices to agree on the outcome of this controversial case. Such unity was quite remarkable. Marshall and Bushrod Washington were the only Federalists remaining on the Court. The other Justices, William Johnson, [Henry] Brockholst Livingston, Thomas Todd, Gabriel Duvall, and Joseph Story, had been appointed by Republican presidents. These Justices might have been expected to oppose the Bank. After all, Republicans championed the return of power to the states at the expense of the national government.

On March 6, the Chief Justice announced the Court's decision. Marshall defended Congress's power to make laws covering a wide range of subjects. Of course, he could have limited himself to the immediate problem of the Bank. All his life, however, the Chief Justice had firmly supported a strong national government. This case offered him another opportunity to speak out for his beliefs. He found fault with the case Maryland's lawyers had made. The existence of the Bank was not an abuse of national power. Congress was not taking for itself powers that were reserved to the states under the Tenth Amendment.

Marshall scolded the states for trying to run the national government. They no longer had such control. To make this point, the Chief Justice compared government under the Articles of Confederation with government under the Constitution. The Articles were an agreement among independent states. Under the Constitution, the states gave up much of their freedom of action to a national government. The people of the United States, not the states, had approved the Constitution in conventions called in each state. Thus "the government of the Union . . . is emphatically, and truly, a government of the people."[26] It certainly was not an agreement among states. What's more, the Constitution became "the supreme law of the land"; state government officials had to take an oath to support it.[27] As a result, states had to accept laws and organizations Congress created.

According to Marshall, the founders wrote, "a constitution intended to endure for ages to come, and consequently, to be adapted to the various crises of human affairs."[28] They did not list every possible circumstance or power. If they had, the Constitution "would probably never be understood by the public. Its nature, therefore, requires that only its great outlines should be marked, its important objects designated, . . ."[29]

This is why the founders gave Congress implied, or unlisted, powers. The Constitution defines implied powers as "Laws which shall be necessary and proper for carrying into execution the foregoing [listed] powers."[30] The Tenth Amendment did not take away Congress's implied powers. It did say powers "not delegated to the United States, nor prohibited to the states, are reserved to the states . . ."[31] It did not distinguish between listed and unlisted powers.

However, the national government could not do whatever it pleased. Its powers were limited. Having limited power, however, did not prevent Congress from having implied powers. According to Marshall, the limits were quite broad.

> Let the end be legitimate, let it be within the scope of the constitution, and all means which are appropriate, which are plainly adapted to that end, which are not prohibited, but consist with the letter and spirit of the constitution, are constitutional.[32]

In other words, Congress could pass laws under its implied powers. These laws had to carry out goals stated in the Constitution. They could not violate specific rules written in the Constitution. The law setting up the second National Bank of the United States met these conditions. Congress

These judicial robes were worn by Chief Justice John Marshall. He believed very deeply in the power of the Constitution. He also believed that the interpretation of the Constitution could and should change with the times.

created the Bank to borrow money and control the currency. These were two powers, or goals, listed in the Constitution.

Marshall then took up Maryland's right to tax the Bank. He restated Webster's argument, "That the power of taxing it [the bank] by the states may be exercised so as to destroy it, is too obvious to be denied."[33] Federal laws were supreme under the Constitution. States had no right to pass tax laws that interfered with the operation of federal laws. The people of a single state could not give the state the power to tax an organization created on behalf of the people of all the states for the benefit of all.

Marshall's decision upset many Americans opposed to the Bank. Newspapers all over the country carried lengthy attacks on the Chief Justice's opinion. Marshall usually did not defend his judgments in public. This time, however, Bushrod Washington urged him to answer his opponents. The Chief Justice wrote a series of essays, published in the _Philadelphia Union_ and in the _Alexandria Gazette_. He reminded the readers that hardly anyone protested at the time the Bank was set up. He also pointed out that members of the Supreme Court would not derive any personal advantage from the decision. They were impartial in their judgments.[34]

Southerners especially resented the Chief Justice's decision. They feared that the national government would turn Marshall's decision against them. The government might use its implied powers to prevent the spread of slavery in states wishing to enter the Union. At the time, Missouri, a slave state, wanted to join the United States. Fortunately, in 1820 both Maine and Missouri were admitted to the Union. The balance between slave and free states was preserved.

President Andrew Jackson took steps to close the Bank in 1832. It went out of existence in 1836. Nevertheless,

McCulloch v. *Maryland* became a landmark decision. It made sure that Congress would have enough power to make the laws a growing country needed. It protected federal government organizations from state taxation. On the other hand, it sparked further debate between supporters of a strong national government and defenders of states' rights. The debate continues to this day.

A Nationalist's Lasting Impact on His Country

Americans still benefit from John Marshall's landmark decisions. His judgments helped shape the present-day government of the United States. The Constitution could not cover every possible situation. It contained many blanks for Marshall and those who came after him to fill in. Marshall's interpretations of the Constitution helped to strengthened national government.

His landmark decision in *Marbury* v. *Madison* helped make the Court an independent and powerful branch of government. It gave the Supreme Court the right to judge the actions of Congress through judicial review. After Marshall's death, however, it looked like judicial review would be forgotten. The Justices did not declare another act of Congress unconstitutional until 1857. Nevertheless, if Marshall had not acted when he did, it might have been impossible for later courts to claim the power to overturn laws passed by Congress.[1]

In 1803, Marshall's decision in *Marbury* v. *Madison* was pretty much taken for granted by the public and politicians. Some Americans, however, were not prepared to accept it. Among them was Judge Gibson in Pennsylvania. In 1825, he presented a series of classic arguments against judicial review.[2] 1) The Constitution did not mention judicial review. As a result, the Supreme Court had no right to pass judgment on the national lawmakers. 2) The national government was divided into three equal and independent branches: the president, the lawmakers, and the judges. Judicial review made the Court superior to the other branches. This violated the Constitution. 3) All government officials took an oath to defend and protect the Constitution. Why should the Supreme Court decide what is constitutional and what is not? Unlike other officials, the Justices were not elected to office. They were not accountable to the voters. Why should they make such important decisions? Judicial review gave the Court too much power.

Some modern government officials have presented similar arguments against judicial review. They have questioned the Supreme Court's right to judge their actions or the validity of the laws they put into effect. Judicial review has been challenged in legal disputes concerning an Arkansas governor's opposition to the racial desegregation of schools,[3] the exclusion of a lawmaker from the House of Representatives,[4] and a president's right to withhold information needed to press criminal charges against members of his staff.[5] In these cases and others, the Justices have successfully defended their right to interpret the Constitution and decide whether laws and actions of government officials are valid. To support their claim, they have relied on Marshall's reasoning in the case of *Marbury* v. *Madison.*

John Marshall did not share Judge Gibson's fear that judicial review would make the Court too powerful. He had already insisted that the powers of the Court were limited. "Judicial power, as contradistinguished from the power of the laws, has no existence. Courts are mere instruments of the law, and can will nothing."[6] Courts could only hear legal disputes brought for judgment. They could not pass judgment on laws at random. So judicial review of national and state laws was limited. What's more, the courts depended on elected officials to carry out their judgments. They might refuse to do so. For example, President Andrew Jackson defied Chief Justice Marshall and banished the Cherokees.[7]

By overruling Supreme Court decisions, amendments to the Constitution have also limited the effects of judicial review. This happened even before Marshall became Chief Justice. In 1793, the Justices had decided that two citizens from South Carolina could sue the state of Georgia in federal court.[8] The citizens wanted to recover property Georgia had taken away from them. Many states were outraged. They resented the loss of their powers under the new Constitution. In 1795, they passed the Eleventh Amendment to prevent citizens of other states or foreign countries from suing a state in federal court. An amendment was used again in 1913 to set aside a Court decision when the Justices overturned an 1894 congressional law to tax earnings. The Sixteenth Amendment was added to the Constitution to allow the government to collect income taxes.

Changing the membership of the Supreme Court has influenced Court decisions, too. Justices eventually die or retire. Presidents try to choose replacements with viewpoints similar to their own. They hope the new Justices will use judicial review to protect their achievements or judge their actions favorably. For example, John Adams originally chose John Marshall as Chief Justice to keep the Court under Federalist control. During the 1930s, President Franklin D. Roosevelt even threatened to increase the size of the Court to win approval for his programs. At that time, the nation's economy had collapsed in the Great Depression. Congress had passed a number of laws to keep businesses operating, to help farmers, and to get people back to work. The Supreme Court declared these laws unconstitutional. The Justices were criticized for defending their own old-fashioned theories of economics. They were accused of ignoring the wishes of the public and its lawmakers. Roosevelt hoped to get the Court to cooperate by appointing more Justices, but such drastic action was not needed. Under pressure from the president, the Court reversed itself and began to uphold the new laws.[9] This example also illustrates another way the effects of judicial review can be limited. The Court can change its mind and overturn previous decisions.

Of course, to prevent a president from using his appointment power to influence court decisions, the Justices may postpone retirement. Marshall was reluctant to leave the choice of a new Chief Justice to President Andrew Jackson. He disagreed with most of the president's programs. In June 1831, he wrote to his friend Justice Joseph Story: "You know how much importance I attach to the character of the person who is to succeed me . . ."[10] He decided to stay on the Court until Jackson left office. Marshall was not able to carry out his plan, however. He died before Jackson's term ended. Since then, other justices have tried to follow John Marshall's

89

example. Illness and death have sometimes defeated their plans, too.

Despite these limits, judicial review has stood the test of time. Between 1803 and 1990, the Supreme Court rejected 125 congressional laws.[11] That averaged to less than one law a year. In doing so, the Court has sometimes slowed and sometimes hastened changes in American life. On the other hand, 1,074 state laws were found to be unconstitutional during the same period.[12] By overturning these state laws, the Supreme Court has helped to give the American people the same justice no matter where they lived.

Like *Marbury* v. *Madison,* John Marshall's landmark decision in *McCulloch* v. *Maryland* has also stood the test of time and has helped to strengthen the national government. The nation's lawmakers have used implied powers to pass laws on subjects the authors of the Constitution never imagined. For example, the federal government now protects the environment, makes sure that food and medicines are safe, and sets speed limits on national highways. Congress has created government organizations to fund scientific research, to license radio stations and television channels, to ensure equal employment opportunity, and even to land a man on the moon. As long as the lawmakers carry out the Constitution's goals and follow its rules, the Supreme Court will not overturn their actions.

McCulloch v. *Maryland* also granted the federal government immunity, or protection, from state taxes. For sixty years, starting in the 1870s, certain private individuals also received this privilege. They claimed immunity because they had a close connection with the federal government. One absurd example was inventors. They received federal patents for their discoveries. (Patents give inventors exclusive control

This seated portrait of John Marshall in old age was painted by James
Hubbard around 1834.

over the use of their discoveries for a fixed period of time.) They did not have to pay state taxes on the money they received for use of their inventions.[13] Since then, the Court has granted immunity from state taxes only to the federal government and federal organizations, such as veterans' hospitals. Employees of the federal government, such as FBI agents, must pay state taxes. Thanks to John Marshall's decision, however, people who buy United States savings bonds do not have to pay state taxes on their earnings.

Chief Justice John Marshall left the American people an important legacy. During his years as Chief Justice, he heard a total of 1,215 cases. The Court did not give opinions in 109 of these cases. Of the remaining 1,106, Marshall wrote 519 decisions and offered nine dissents.[14] (Today, the Supreme Court disposes of about 175 cases a year.[15]) John Marshall's landmark decisions have had a lasting effect on American society. His other major decisions influenced American history as well.

Marshall's judgments made it possible for large corporations to develop. He protected the contracts they signed from changes demanded by state lawmakers. For a time, this gave corporations a chance to grow without government interference. He also removed obstacles to their doing business in more than one state. Thus he helped the United States to become one huge market for corporations' products, rather than a series of individual state markets.

Not only did he encourage the growth of American commerce and industry, but he also protected the rights of property owners. State lawmakers could not take away their lands by breaking agreements they had signed. Governments as well as private citizens had to keep their promises. Marshall hoped this would produce an orderly and free society. Away

The Supreme Court's basement chamber, under the senate, was restored in 1976 to look as it did in John Marshall's day.

from his judicial duties, he also protected property owners by defending voting qualifications that let them take part in elections, but denied the right to vote to many Americans. Marshall did not want to make the United States a more democratic nation. He did not welcome changes that increased the number of voters or that led political parties to make emotional appeals to the public for support. On the other hand, as Chief Justice, he used his position to help minorities. Unfortunately, he could only teach and preach. He could not change the way Americans behaved toward African Americans and Native Americans, for example.

In his day, Chief Justice John Marshall was sometimes seen as a determined Federalist. After all, John Adams had appointed him to the Supreme Court to preserve the Federalist party's views of government. Some of Marshall's decisions certainly reflected the party's values. For example, *Marbury* v. *Madison* can be regarded as a Federalist Justice's attempt to embarrass President Jefferson and the Republican party. Aaron Burr's acquittal on treason charges also challenged the Republican president and his supporters. These decisions, however, were not just political judgments. They established important ideas about the process of judicial review and treason.

It is perhaps more accurate to say that Marshall was a nationalist. His desire to strengthen the national government led him to join the Federalist party. After the party dissolved in 1812, he continued to work toward limiting the influence of the states, making the federal government more powerful, and preserving the independence of the federal courts. He was committed to these goals throughout his life.

John Marshall brought about the realization of the hopes and dreams of the nation's founders. Under his leadership, the

The modern court room of the Supreme Court looks like this today.

Constitution became more than a list of limits on government powers. It became a flexible set of rules to guide future generations. Marshall insisted that both the national and state governments obey these rules. He also made sure that the laws were fair and protected ordinary citizens. He made the Supreme Court the guardian of the Constitution. The Justices alone could interpret its words. As a result, the Court became an important branch of government. Because of his many accomplishments, Americans past and present have admired and respected Chief Justice John Marshall as an outstanding judge and an American patriot.

Chronology

September 24, 1755—John Marshall's birth.

1775—Volunteered to serve in War of Independence.

Winter of 1777–1778—Stationed at Valley Forge with George Washington.

May–July 1780—Studied law at The College of William and Mary.

August 28, 1780—Admitted to the Virginia Bar.

February 12, 1781—Retired from the Continental Army.

1782—Elected to the Virginia House of Delegates for the first time.

January 3, 1783—Married Mary Willis "Polly" Ambler.

1784—Appointed as a Councillor of State.

1787—Elected to the Virginia House of Delegates.

1788—Elected to Virginia Constitutional Convention.

1789—Elected to the Virginia House of Delegates.

1795—Elected to the Virginia House of Delegates.

1796—Argued *Ware* v. *Hylton* before the Supreme Court.

1797—Mission to France—XYZ affair.

1799—Elected to the U.S. House of Representatives.

1800—Appointed secretary of state.

January 27, 1801—Became Chief Justice of the United States Supreme Court.

1803—*Marbury* v. *Madison.*

1807—Presided over treason trial of Aaron Burr.

1810—*Fletcher* v. *Peck.*

1819—*McCulloch* v. *Maryland.*

1819—*Trustees of Dartmouth College* v. *Woodward.*

1824—*Gibbons* v. *Ogden.*

1829—Served as delegate to the Virginia Convention to change the state constitution.

December 25, 1831—Death of Polly Marshall.

1832—*Worcester* v. *Georgia.*

July 6, 1835—Marshall's death.

Chapter Notes

Chapter 1

1. Until the 22nd Amendment to the Constitution was passed in 1933, the incoming president and Congress were sworn in in March, not January as is done today.

2. David Loth, *John Marshall and the Growth of the Republic* (New York: W.W. Norton & Company, Inc., 1949), p. 190.

3. John A. Garraty, "The Case of the Missing Commissions," *Quarrels That Have Shaped the Constitution*, ed. John A. Garraty, rev. ed. (New York: Harper & Row Publishers, 1987), p. 10.

4. The Constitution set up the national government. It divided the government into three branches: the presidency, the lawmakers, and the judges. It described their powers and placed limits on what they could do. It also defined relations between the states and the national government and limited their powers.

5. Members of the Supreme Court are called Justices, not judges.

6. Albert J. Beveridge, *The Life of John Marshall*, 4 vols. (Boston: Houghton Mifflin Company, 1916), Vol. III, p. 122.

7. Ibid.

8. Currently the Supreme Court meets from October to June.

9. United States Constitution, Article II, Section 4.

Chapter 2

1. Frances North Mason, *My Dearest Polly: Letters of Chief Justice John Marshall* (Richmond: Garrett & Massie, 1961), p. 202.

2. Allan B. Magruder, *John Marshall* (Boston: Houghton, Mifflin and Company, 1899), p. 9.

3. Francis N. Stites, *John Marshall: Defender of the Constitution* (Boston: Little, Brown and Company, 1981), p. 7.

4. Magruder, pp. 10–11.

5. David Loth, *John Marshall and the Growth of the Republic* (New York: W.W. Norton & Company, Inc., 1949), p. 31.

6. Ibid., p. 41.

7. Albert J. Beveridge, *The Life of John Marshall*, 4 vols. (Boston: Houghton Mifflin Company, 1916), Vol I, p. 118.

8. Leonard Baker, *John Marshall: A Life in Law* (New York: Macmillan, 1974), p. 46.

9. Beveridge, pp. 150–151.

10. Loth, p. 54.

11. Mason, p. 6.

12. Mason, pp. 343–344.

13. Stites, p. 18.

14. Samuel Konefsky, *John Marshall and Alexander Hamilton: Architects of the American Constitution* (New York: Macmillan, 1964), p. 254.

15. Ibid., p. 73.

16. Stites, p. 27.

17. Edward S. Corwin, *John Marshall and the Constitution* (New York: United States Publishers, Inc., 1977), p. 218.

18. Mason, pp. 308–309.

19. Ibid., p. 96.

20. Ibid., p. 121.

21. Corwin, p. 212.

22. Baker, p. 521.

23. Ibid., p. 10.

24. Magruder, p. 267.

25. Mason, p. 250.

26. Corwin, pp. 221–222.

27. Beveridge, Vol. IV, p. 526.

Chapter 3

1. Francis N. Stites, *John Marshall: Defender of the Constitution* (Boston: Little, Brown and Company, 1981), p. 23.

2. Lord Craigmyle, *John Marshall in Diplomacy and in Law* (New York: Charles Scribner's Sons, 1933), p. 11.

3. Frances North Mason, *My Dearest Polly: Letters of Chief Justice John Marshall* (Richmond, Va.: Garrett & Massie, 1961), p. 71.

4. Albert J. Beveridge, *The Life of John Marshall,* 4 vols. (Boston: Houghton Mifflin Company, 1916), Vol. II, p. 177.

5. Ibid., Vol. II, p. 201. The current value of Marshall's earnings, purchases, and salary as a Justice mentioned in this book was calculated for the author by the Bureau of Labor Statistics, Department of Labor.

6. Ibid., p. 187.

7. Stites, p. 53.

8. Ibid., p. 24.

9. Arthur N. Holcombe, "John Marshall as Politician and Political Theorist," in *Chief Justice John Marshall: A Reappraisal,* ed. W. Melville Jones (Ithaca: Cornell University Press, 1956), p. 33.

10. Mason, p. 52.

11. Leonard Baker, *John Marshall: A Life in Law* (New York: Macmillan, 1964), p. 118.

12. David Loth, *John Marshall and the Growth of the Republic* (New York: W.W. Norton & Company, Inc., 1949), p. 104.

13. Ibid., p. 78.

14. Beveridge, Vol. II, pp. 33–34.

15. Loth, p. 120.

16. Baker, p. 215.

17. Ibid., p. 217.

18. Beveridge, Vol. II, p. 211.

19. Baker, p. 218.

20. Loth, pp. 127–128.

21. Craigmyle, p. 70.

22. Baker, p. 255.

23. Ibid., p. 247.

24. Stites, p. 61.

25. Loth, pp. 138–139.

26. Baker, p. 260.

27. Beveridge, Vol. II, p. 348.

28. Loth, p. 150.

29. Charles Fairman, "John Marshall and the American Judicial Tradition," in *Chief Justice John Marshall: A Reappraisal*, ed. W. Melville Jones (Ithaca: Cornell University Press, 1956), p. 91.

30. Beveridge, Vol. II, p. 407.

31. Mason, p. 136.

32. Allan B. Magruder, *John Marshall* (Boston: Houghton Mifflin and Company, 1899), p. 148.

32. Magruder, p. 148.

33. Mason, p. 141.

34. Baker, p. 332.

35. Irving Brant, "John Marshall and The Lawyers and Politicians," in *Chief Justice John Marshall: A Reappraisal*, ed. W. Melville Jones (Ithaca: Cornell University Press, 1956), p. 47.

Chapter 4

1. David Loth, *John Marshall and the Growth of the Republic* (New York: W.W. Norton & Company, Inc., 1949) p. 158.

2. Charles Fairman, "John Marshall and the American Judicial Tradition," in *Chief Justice John Marshall: A Reappraisal*, ed. W. Melville Jones (Ithaca: Cornell University Press, 1956), p. 82.

3. The current value of Marshall's salary as a Justice was calculated for the author by the Bureau of Labor Statistics, Department of Labor.

4. *The World Almanac 1994* (New York: Funk & Wagnalls, 1993), p. 84.

5. Loth, p. 162.

6. Frances North Mason, *My Dearest Polly: Letters of Chief Justice John Marshall* (Richmond, Va.: Garrett & Massie, 1961), p. 297.

7. Albert J. Beveridge, *The Life of John Marshall*, 4 vols. (Boston: Houghton Mifflin Company, 1916), Vol. IV, p. 81.

8. Mason, p. 220.

9. Loth, p. 275.

10. Fairman, p. 97; Arthur N. Holcombe, "John Marshall as Politician and Political Theorist," in *Chief Justice John Marshall: A*

Reappraisal, ed. W. Melville Jones (Ithaca, N.Y.: Cornell University Press, 1956), p. 82.

11. Mason, pp. 315–316.

12. Edward S. Corwin, *John Marshall and the Constitution* (New York: United States Publishers, Inc., 1977), p. 218.

13. Ibid.

14. Ibid., p. 199–200.

15. Leonard Baker, *John Marshall: A Life in Law* (New York: Macmillan, 1974), p. 455.

16. Mason, p. 186.

17. Baker, p. 495.

18. Ibid., p. 480.

19. Ibid., p. 486.

20. Francis N. Stites, *John Marshall: Defender of the Constitution* (Boston: Little Brown and Company, 1981), p. 107.

21. Corwin, p. 210.

22. Baker, p. 531.

23. *Fletcher* v. *Peck,* 6 Cranch 87 (1810).

24. *Trustees of Dartmouth College* v. *Woodward* 4 Wheaton 518 (1819).

25. *Gibbons* v. *Ogden* 9 Wheaton 1 (1824).

26. Ibid., pp. 190.

27. Ibid., p. 194.

28. Beveridge, Vol. IV, p. 473.

29. Baker, p. 645.

30. *The Antelope* 10 Wheaton, 114 (1825).

31. *Boyce* v. *Anderson* 2 Peters 150–156 (1829).

32. Corwin, p. 194.

33. Loth, p. 360.

34. *Cherokee Nation* v. *Georgia* 5 Peters 1 (1831).

35. Baker, p. 739.

36. Beveridge, Vol. IV, p. 543.

37. *Worcester* v. *Georgia* 6 Peters 515 (1832).

38. Ibid., p. 561.

39. Loth, p. 365.

40. Baker, p. 549.

Chapter 5

1. Allan B. Magruder, *John Marshall* (Boston: Houghton Mifflin and Company, 1899), p. 166.

2. Francis N. Stites, *John Marshall: Defender of the Constitution* (Boston: Little, Brown and Company, 1981), p. 87.

3. Leonard Baker, *John Marshall: A Life in Law* (New York: Macmillan, 1974), p. 401.

4. 1 Cranch 154 (1803).

5. Ibid., p. 159.

6. Ibid., p. 170.

7. Ibid., p. 174.

8. Magruder, pp. 82–83.

9. 1 Cranch 179 (1803).

10. Ibid., p. 177.

11. Ibid., pp. 178–179.

12. Albert J. Beveridge, *The Life of John Marshall,* 4 vols. (Boston: Houghton Mifflin Company, 1916), Vol III, p. 153.

13. Edward S. Corwin, *John Marshall and the Constitution* (New York: United States Publishers, Inc., 1977), pp. 11-12.

14. Gerald Gunther, *Constitutional Law,* 12th ed. (Westbury, New York: The Foundation Press, Inc., 1991), p. 15.

15. Corwin, p. 62.

16. 1 Cranch 177 (1803).

17. The current value of the tax mentioned in this book was calculated for the author by the Bureau of Labor Statistics, Department of Labor.

18. Gunther, p. 83.

19. Wheaton 426 (1819).

20. Ibid., p. 323.

21. Ibid., p. 327.

22. David Loth, *John Marshall and the Growth of the Republic* (New York: W. W. Norton & Company, Inc., 1949), p. 303.

23. 4 Wheaton 374 (1819).

24. Samuel Konefsky, *John Marshall and Alexander Hamilton: Architects of the American Constitution* (New York: Macmillan, 1964), p. 170.

25. Beveridge, Vol. IV, pp. 90-91.

26. 4 Wheaton 404–405 (1819).

27. Ibid., p. 406.

28. Ibid., p. 415.

29. Ibid., p. 407.

30. Ibid., p. 412.

31. Ibid., p. 406.

32. Ibid., p. 421.

33. Ibid., p. 427.

34. Baker, pp. 605–615.

Chapter 6

1. Samuel Konefsky, *John Marshall and Alexander Hamilton: Architects of the American Constitution* (New York: Macmillan, 1964), p. 90.

2. *Eakin* v. *Raub*, 12 Sargeant and Rawle 30 (Pa. 1825).

3. *Cooper* v. *Aaron* 358 US 1 (1958).

4. *Powell* v. *McCormack* 395 US 486 (1969).

5. *United States* v. *Nixon* 418 US 683 (1974).

6. *Osborn* v. *Bank of the United States* 9 Wheaton 866 (1824).

7. See Chapter 5.

8. *Chisholm* v. *Georgia*, 2 Dall. (2 US) 419 (1793).

9. For example, *NLRB* v. *Jones & Laughlin* 301 US 1 (1937).

10. Konefsky, p. 236.

11. *Supplement to Annotations of Cases Decided by the Supreme Court of the United States* (Washington, D.C.: Government Printing Office, 1991), p. 242.

12. Ibid., p. 259.

13. *Long* v. *Rockwood*, 277 US 142 (1928).

14. David Loth, *John Marshall and the Growth of the Republic* (New York: W.W. Norton & Company, Inc., 1949), p. 376.

15. U.S. Department of Commerce, Bureau of the Census, *Statistical Abstract of the United States 1991*, 111th ed. (Washington, D.C.: Government Printing Office, 1991), p. 189.

Glossary

amendments to the Constitution—Changes to the Constitution. They are made by adding new ideas and/or eliminating old ones. To amend the Constitution requires a proposal from two-thirds Congress or state lawmaking bodies. This must be approved by three-quarters of the state lawmaking bodies or special meetings within the states.

attorney general—The official responsible for arguing the government's side in lawsuits; also the head of the Department of Justice which was established in 1870.

bail—Money deposited with the court to insure that a person will appear for trial.

bribery—Taking money for doing a political favor.

Chief Justice of the United States—The head of the Supreme Court.

circuit courts—Federal courts that hear appeals from trial courts.

Congress—The nation's lawmakers. They are divided into two bodies: the House of Representatives and the Senate.

Constitution—The document that set up the national government of the United States. It divided the government into three branches: the presidency, the lawmakers, and the judges. It described their powers and placed limits on what they could do. It also defined relations between the states and the national government and limited their powers.

contract—An agreement to do or not to do something.

convention—A formal meeting of delegates (people who represent the entire membership of an organization).

council of state—A group of men who advised the governor of Virginia on programs and appointments to state offices.

espionage—A secret plot against the government that involves spies.

federal district judges—Officials who preside over trial courts and hear a case for the first time.

grand jury—A panel that decides whether a person should be charged with a crime.

immunity—Protection, for example, immunity from taxes offers protection against having to pay them.

implied powers—Congress's general right to make laws that are necessary and proper to carry out its specific responsibilities listed in the Constitution.

jurisdiction—The power, authority, or range of control over others; the right of the Supreme Court to hear certain types of cases.

Justices—The title given to judges who are members of the United States Supreme Court.

justices of the peace—Officials who settle minor disputes and issue court orders.

monopoly—Exclusive rights to sell or make a product or service which prevents competition by others.

nationalist—An American who viewed the United States as a whole, not just from the perspective of an individual state where he or she lived.

nullify—To reject or cancel (a law).

opinions—The decisions, or judgments, of the Supreme Court of the United States.

police powers—Control over public health and safety.

political parties—Organizations that put up candidates for office at election time and may have different views about the way government should be run.

privateers—Privately owned, armed vessels that governments permitted to attack the nation's enemies.

ratification—A formal process of voting used to approve the Constitution and amendments to it.

repeal—To cancel or take back. The Repeal Act of 1802 canceled the Judiciary Act of 1801.

Supreme Court—The nation's highest court. It hears appeals from other federal courts and from state courts.

tariffs—Fees paid to the government on goods brought in from abroad for sale in the country.

treason—Actions betraying one's country.

writ of mandamus—A court order requiring a government official to perform his or her lawful duties.

Further Reading

Buskie, Morris. ed. *Significant American Colonial Leaders*. Chicago: Children's Press, 1975.

Curtin, Andrew. *Gallery of Great Americans*. New York: Franklin Watts, Inc., 1965.

Flynn, James C. *Famous Justices of the Supreme Court*. New York: Dodd, 1968.

Foley, Ray. *Famous Makers of America*. New York: Dodd, 1963.

Friedman, Leonard. *The Supreme Court*. New York: Chelsea House, 1987.

Garraty, John A., ed. *Quarrels That Have Shaped the Constitution*. rev. ed. New York: Harper & Row, 1987.

Marquardt, Dorothy A. *A Guide to the Supreme Court*. Indianapolis: Bobbs-Merrill, 1977.

Monsell, Helen Albee. *John Marshall: Boy of Young America*. Indianapolis: Bobbs-Merrill, 1949.

Index

J

Jackson, Andrew, 55, 57, 88, 89
Jay, John, 54
Jay Treaty of 1794, 42, 51
Jefferson, Thomas, 6, 7, 8, 10, 21,
    36, 40, 52, 57, 58, 60, 62, 72
Jockey Club, 32
Johnson, William, 81
Jones, Walter, 79
Judiciary Act of 1801, 7, 10

K

Keith, Mary Randolph, 16

L

Lafayette, Marquis de, 19, 41
Lee, Charles, 12
Lincoln, General Levi, 12
Livingston, (Henry) Brockholst,
    81
Louisiana Territory, 77

M

McCulloch, James W., 78
McCulloch v. *Maryland*, 79, 85, 90
Madison, James, 8, 10, 27, 39,
    57, 63, 72, 73
Marbury v. *Madison*, 12, 72,
    76-77, 80, 86-88, 90, 94
Marbury, William, 5-8, 10, 11,
Marshall, James, 6, 14
Marshall, Polly, 33, 34
Marshall, Thomas, 15, 16, 22
Martin, Luther, 79
Martineau, Harriet, 32
Mason, George, 39
Minutemen, 19
Mississippi, Natchez, 62
Monmouth, Battle of, 20
Monroe, James, 19, 27, 36, 38, 57
Moore, Alfred, 73

N

National Bankruptcy Act, 51
New Orleans, 62

P

patents, 90
Paterson, William, 53-54, 73
Phi Beta Kappa, 21
Philadelphia, 43
Philadelphia Union, 84
Pickering, John, 11
Pickering, Timothy, 43
Pinckney, Charles Cotesworth,
    42, 44
Pinckney, William, 79, 80
Proclamation of Neutrality, 41
Proclamation of 1763, 17

Q

Quoit Club, 32

R

Repeal Act, 10, 11
Republicans, 6, 7, 8, 10, 11, 52
Revolution of 1789, 40
Richmond Circulating Library, 32
Richmond City Jail, 60
Robbins Affair, 51
Roosevelt, Franklin D., 89

S

Second Bank of the United States,
    77, 82
Shays, Daniel, 38
Shays Rebellion, 38, 40
"Silverheels", 20
Sixteenth Amendment, 88
Sixth Congress, 50
Slaughter, Captain Philip, 20
slavery, 67, 69, 84
Society of the Cincinnati, 32